Scammed in America

by Dorothy Harding

DORRANCE PUBLISHING CO
EST. 1920
PITTSBURGH, PENNSYLVANIA 15238

The contents of this work, including, but not limited to, the accuracy of events, people, and places depicted; opinions expressed; permission to use previously published materials included; and any advice given or actions advocated are solely the responsibility of the author, who assumes all liability for said work and indemnifies the publisher against any claims stemming from publication of the work.

All Rights Reserved
Copyright © 2021 by Dorothy Harding

No part of this book may be reproduced or transmitted, downloaded, distributed, reverse engineered, or stored in or introduced into any information storage and retrieval system, in any form or by any means, including photocopying and recording, whether electronic or mechanical, now known or hereinafter invented without permission in writing from the publisher.

Dorrance Publishing Co
585 Alpha Drive
Pittsburgh, PA 15238
Visit our website at *www.dorrancebookstore.com*

ISBN: 978-1-6386-7075-9
eISBN: 978-1-6386-7895-3

Scammed in America

★ ★ ★

In 2019 two hundred million dollars were lost to scams. This is according to FTC and FBI. But only 1 percent is officially reported according to FBI. Romance scams are big business. According to FBI, these scams have tripled over last five years. Why are they not reported? There are two victims in these scams: the client, as they are referred to by scammers, and the identity theft victim whose pictures were used to scam the client out of money. Most of these are women, middle aged, widowed, divorced, seeking companionship online.

Millions of people turn to online dating apps or social networking sites to meet someone. But instead of finding romance, many find a scammer trying to trick them into sending money. Romance scammers create fake profiles usually with stolen photos from other unsuspecting people usually off of social media sites: Facebook or Instagram. Some will actually contact women through social media sites: Facebook, Instagram or Google Hangouts. Some even use Words with Friends to meet women to scam. They start a relationship with women to build trust and then talk for hours a day providing a structure of trust by quickly professing their love and attachment usually within weeks. Then they make up a story, usually an emergency, to say that they need money. I was a victim of this romance scam. This is my story. Most people say, "Why would you send anyone money? Why would you fall for someone you never met?" By telling my story, I am allowing you to see the victim's story.

The process that was used to lure me into his scam. Most do not report this crime. Why? They are embarrassed, ashamed of themselves, and hide info from family. Most are traumatized and emotionally devastated. Why am I speaking out? I watched an exposé on a woman in Canada who was an intelligent, hardworking, good person who was lured in and lost two million dollars to scammers.

Dorothy Harding

She sold everything, home, furniture, jewelry, and in the end, they wanted more. They convinced her she was in legal trouble, and with this, she could not handle it. She committed suicide! This beautiful soul was scammed by several men and eventually gave up her life. I realized this could be any middle-aged woman, including me. So I reported my scam to FBI and started my journey to learn more of this subject. How did this happen to me? Why? How many others are there? I wanted answers to all my questions. I wanted to know who this person who lied to me for almost a year was. This is my story, and I have changed my name to protect me. I will use the fake name the scammer used so others can see if they have fallen victim to him. I know of two other women so far. These conversations are through texts, phone calls. Because I have filed a complaint, I was asked to save them as proof.

I also have literally thousands of photos too. These were stolen from a professional businessman whom I will not name for his protection. As I tell my story, I will feed in knowledgeable information I have gained over the last several months of investigating romance scams. Hopefully it will provide answers to the reader's questions. This book is serving as form of therapy for me even though I have not received the answers I require as to why me? It shows how it can happen to anyone.

Most of my references are public. You can google Romance Scams, Yahoo Boys, or visit websites. FBI has an Internet Crime Complaint Center (IC3.gov) to make a complaint or to get more information. I found more internet info from the website Scamhaters United LTD (where I found my scammer); a wealth of information is based in UK. Scamwatch.gov is an Australia-based website that is very informative. There is a advocatingforu.com, who advocates against romance scammers, helping legislate reform to protect others from becoming victims. What most people don't understand is that once you are a victim, you are subject to other forms of scamming. The personal info I provided to this scammer can be bought and sold within their group or to other criminal entities. I personally have been bombarded with scammers by text, email, and phone calls. The other victim is the man, in my case, whose pictures were stolen. It has been since 2017 that his pictures were first used, but if they are productive with them, the scammers buy and sell them to other scammers. He will be a continuous victim also. I know his true identity but will never divulge it.

I dedicate this book to all the victims of Romance Scams and hope to provide some information to the readers. I hear, "Why would you give money to someone you never met? Are you stupid and gullible! It's all your fault this happened to you!" These scammers are professional criminals; they spend days and nights providing productive storylines to victims to hook you into a relationship.

These criminals, if good, scam hundreds of thousands of dollars out of unsuspecting victims. I know mine had at least two other victims on the hook at the same time as me. It's not you and him; it's you and them. Most victims are humiliated, embarrassed, and too damaged to speak but will speak to another. We want to forget and move on, but most need therapy, and some even attempt suicide! These women are middle-aged professionals, divorced, or widows who worked hard for everything they have in life. The other victims are professional businessmen, military, celebrities whose photos are used to lure and manipulate victims. We are survivors who had no idea scammers existed in this form. I hope this book is a form of education to those who read it and a warning to prevent others from becoming a victim. I wish to break the stigma most victims have been categorized as stupid and gullible. We are human, and our mistakes will scar us for life. Please be kind to any victim, because until you have walked in their shoes, you have no idea what they had to go through to survive.

Most of the other victims I have talked to are wonderful, intelligent, and beautiful women. They are sometimes leery of speaking about their ordeal. I can honestly say I was shocked by not only what happened to me but how bad this actually has gotten. This is happening all over the world and for years. United Kingdom, Sweden, The Philippines, Australia, Canada, Germany, France have all had issues. They approach their victims on Facebook, Instagram, Words with Friends, all dating sites. If you are a middle-aged woman and on one of these sites, chances are you will be approached by a scammer multiple times. This is our reality now. How can they be stopped? Educating women on what to watch out for and stopping them from stealing identities from social media. I cannot believe I paid a dating website good money to set me up with a scammer! This should not have happened at all, but this shows how sophisticated these criminals are. They buy and sell fake dating profiles to other criminals. Facebook profiles, Instagram profiles are faked to lure in victims. Most victims are unaware until they lose thousands of dollars they will never see again, and the other victims never knew their photos were stolen until all those women find them and contact them asking where their money is! Recently, here in the United States, several high-profile cases are making headlines because they are expanding into hacking business accounts and stealing large amounts of money from businesses. Unless this happens, there seems to be no justice in any of us victims' cases, but as I talk to other victims, you never give up hope that the scammer who stole money from you will get caught. I have moved forward with my life, and even though it has only been five months since I found out I was involved with a scammer, it is still raw, and the pain and anger may take years to recover. Some of these victims sink into a depression, and some get swallowed up and lose the battle. This book is for them who could not move on! My goal is for each and every middle-aged woman to think before signing up on a dating website or friending some stranger on social media, because you may think it's innocent, but chances are, these scammers are more sinister than you think.

    Winter of 2018 was hard. I had just undergone a major operation to repair a broken neck and was over four years divorced. I needed to make some changes I turned fifty-nine in October and needed a change. I received news my beloved namesake aunt was dying of cancer. I was heartbroken and went for a visit the end of February 2019 to say my goodbyes. She was still alive, and I finally got the okay from my surgeon to travel. I also was thinking about signing up for a dating app, just to see what was out there. I worked midnights and lived forty miles away from nearest relative and needed to step into the new era of dating. I looked around and chose between e-Harmony or Zoosk, both had good reviews. I ended up choosing Zoosk. I signed up in February 2019. At first you choose a fake name to use for animosity, use your own photo and write a description of yourself and what you like and dislike to do and what type of person you are looking for. I spent several weeks swiping through photos and talked to several men, of which none seemed to fit what I was looking for. By the beginning of March 2019, I began to think maybe this was not for me. I received a notice from the dating site; maybe I would consider someone further away outside my area? I swiped yes; why not see if I might have better luck? Within two hours, I swiped this profile of this man, a nice, friendly, middle-aged face businessman. Widowed with two children, loves to travel, everything I was looking for. So I swiped like and sent a heart, and within minutes, I received a heart like back. "Hi, you are beautiful," he said, and I responded that he had a nice, friendly face. By the way, the dating site provides messaging platform so you can talk anonymously without giving out personal info. Within two hours, we made the decision to move to our personal phones. I have call protect on my phone, so I can delete and block a number immediately if I feel threatened. During my story, I will refer to myself as Donna, and his name used is Erick Andersen. This is a fake name, so I feel confident in using this name in my story.

>**Erick:** Hi Donna, this is Erick from Zoosk X. Nice to have you here X What's your plan for the day?
>**Me:** I work midnights so sleep is on the agenda for today.
>**Erick:** What work do you do if you don't mind me asking?
>**Me:** I monitor contracts for the government.
>**Erick:** That is impressive beautiful. I sell and supply hospital instruments and I am a investment specialist. Are you working in your chosen field?
>**Me:** I have worked several occupations throughout my life but this one seems to fit me well.
>**Erick:** Thank you for taking your time to share with me X. Yes, I am self employed and hire some professionals as my team to work more productively and effectively. When do you plan to retire? What do you plan to do when you retire?
>**Me:** I have no plans as of now and I am a few years away from retiring, but I plan on staying busy regardless of retiring. I would love to retire somewhere warm with a beach nearby.
>**Erick:** That is sweet to hear an active mind is a healthy mind. If you could live anywhere in the world, where would it be?
>**Me:** Definitely somewhere warm maybe Florida. I grew up in the Midwest but have a need for warmer climate.
>**Erick:** I have a home in Fisher Island, Miami. Maybe we can spend a weekend there in a time not too far away from now.
>**Me:** I have been to Florida but mostly the northern half not to southern half.

Erick: Have you ever been to the Bahamas?
Me: No, I have been throughout the Caribbean but not to the Bahamas.
Erick: Ok, maybe it is in your book of destiny X. I'm originally from Clayford Hill, Nassau, Bahamas.
Me: Were you raised in the Bahamas?
Erick: Yes, I was raised there by my parents. I came to the states when I was 27 to seek greener pastures. I first lived in NY and still have a home there and then moved to Miami. Do you ever go to NY?
Me: No, I have never been to NY. It must have been shock going from such a warm climate In the Bahamas to a cold climate in NY. I grew up in Detroit so I never wished to visit another huge city. I prefer warmer climates to vacation.
Erick: I moved a lot to accommodate my business growth. What is your religious beliefs?
Me: I grew up going to church every Sunday. My family is Protestant Christian. But I do not attend church services much anymore I am more spiritual now like my mother. I personally believe that all religions have a right to their beliefs and so do I. I believe god does not judge you for whether you attend church or not but your true belief In him. I read the bible and pray regularly.

At this time, I had never heard of romance scams nor had I dated in twenty-one years. I was divorced several years and needed to take the time to concentrate on me and rebuilding my life. I was married for ten and a half years, but we were together for sixteen years. The divorce was devastating for me, and for a simple open and shut divorce, it became a legal war. My ex was extremely controlling and materialistic, and in a state of 50/50, he fought every legal decision made.

So stepping into online dating was very new to me and became uncharted waters to navigate. I truly believed that when you signed up and paid good money to a dating website, you had some protection.

Erick: My father was a preacher and has since passed. All that I have is my mother and step-brother left. I know you have many experiences to share with me. I'm passionate for a world filled with love, peace and forgiveness. I am also passionate about teaching and writing. I love traveling and exploring beautiful places.

Me: Are you writing about traveling?

Erick: I am writing a book about patience. Patience a Virtue is the name of the book I have chosen so far. It's a book that grows with me.

Me: The world needs more love and patience. It's a lost virtue these days.

Erick: Every religion and faith is based on that as a key to peaceful living based on patience and is a practical expression of faith and humility to your creator regardless of how you worship and serve him. Is it important to have your own family home or do you prefer apartment or condo living, with a management company responsible for maintenance? Are you a do it yourselfer or would you rather hire professionals? Do you clean your own home or do you hire a professional?

Me: I have lived in my own home and apartments. I prefer a personal dwelling versus a apartment But I am single now and live alone so an apartment suits me fine. I am a DYI person I love being creative it in my blood. I hire professionals for the big stuff when it comes to home maintenance. I worked previously as a commercial cleaner so I prefer to do all cleaning myself. My father believed that his daughters should learn how to use a hammer and wrench so I grew up learning basic home maintenance.

Erick: I am a DIY man too. But I leave the rest to professionals. I love music and play the drums and Piano but would love to learn the violin. What is your type of music?

Me: I grew up in Motown so I love R&B, Rock and Blues. My parents were Country and Gospel Music lovers. So I was

7

exposed to a wide variety of different genre of music.
Erick: That's nice and music is a source of calmness. Can you play a instrument? Do you have a favorite artist?
Me: I have never played a musical instrument. I have a lot of favorite artists I listen to regularly.
Erick: I like Soft Rock, Pop, R&B, Gospel and Reggae music. I sang in my dad's church while growing up. My mother was my first Sunday School Teacher and Choir Master.
Me: Did your mother sing?
Erick: My father said her voice was the charm that caught his attention.

(He sent a picture of him with his mother. It looked like an older picture to me.)

Me: I see the resemblance between you and your mother.
Erick: I have more of her heart in me. Do you think of your home as a cocoon or is your door always open? What do you need to feel energized and inspired in your home?
Me: I think a home should reflect an individuals taste. It should be stylish and comfortable. I am always energized and inspired in whatever dwelling I am in. Its called being constantly creative. I think your home should reflect your own personal taste.
Erick: A home is where you bring together your spirit, your soul and your body to ignite. I enjoy peace so everything in my world is centered around peaceful ambience and atmosphere. Have you ever felt deeply insecure in a relationship? Were you able to name that fear?
Me: I have never felt insecure in a relationship but I have easily determined whether a relationship will last or not. I am a extrovert so I do not require others opinion to exist. I am comfortable in my own skin with my flaws. I think once you accept yourself as is you eliminate any insecurities. But I

also existed in a marriage that we were both unhappy with. It all about how much your willing to sacrifice for the other.
Erick: That's true it takes maturity and understanding to be honest that is freedom. When You lie it begins to grow step by step, then it begins to grow disappointments and Heartbreak etc. (Another picture arrives via text with him and a boy. It seemed random, when we were talking, when the pictures would arrive.)
Erick: Meet Mark my oldest he is 15 years old! We share the same birthdate.

(A second picture arrives again with him and another boy.)

Erick: Meet Logan my youngest he is 13 years old!
Me: They are both beautiful boys and the youngest looks a lot like you.
Erick: Hahaha, he's the cook and is more academic. Mark is the oldest and is more creative.

More pictures arrived with him and the two boys; some were older pictures, when the boys were younger. Establishing a sentimental attachment is part of the scammer's game. I was unaware of scammers. I was merely trying to get to know someone I just met. Because he stated he was Bahamian, I ignored his responses to answers. If he had used an American profile, I would have questioned his English translation.

Erick: Do you have any photos you would like to share? I sent several recent photos that I had taken within the last several months. I am not Into taking selfies much.
Me: I need to charge my phone it is dying and get in some sleep I have to work again tonight. Can we talk later?
Erick: I have really enjoyed our chats and I miss you already.

Another selfie was sent of himself was sent. Scammers have to establish a connection as soon as possible, so using romance is the best way. They are known for using scripts; it's all preplanned. Social Catfish, an online dating investigation service, shared an actual playbook provided by a member of a Nigerian dating scam ring and provided insight how these scammers operate. There are dozens, if not hundreds, of examples of pre-crafted introductions, questions, and responses meant to slowly trick a victim into falling for a scheme. The idea behind the scripts is to create the feeling of a whirlwind romance, the type of thing you see in a movie. The victim quickly starts to fall for the scammer as they display charm wit, compassion, and kindness. They say all the right things and seem to have their life together. Some talk up their education or financial security to make it seem they do not need anything from their victim or at least have the resources to pay them back.

A series of photos were sent via text; there was also a wedding photo.

>**Me:** Beautiful photos how long were you married?
>**Erick:** Me and my late wife were married 22 years. How was your day?
>**Me:** I have been busy with phone calls and personal business and did not sleep much.
>**Erick:** I have been busy also and looking forward with excitement to communicate with You.
>**Me:** You mentioned you have a step-brother?
>**Erick:** My brother lives in NY and he is a brand developer and life coach who also does some work for me. Praises to our creator that he keeps his promises, he impacts each and everyone of us with the right tools to run your race. Are you an emotional person?
>**Me:** I am a strong person who does well under pressure but I can become emotional when it involves my love ones. Or if I am passionate about something I tend to get emotional.
>**Erick:** The best clothes that impress me is the beautiful colors of your mind and your heart. because the value of a person is not what they have, their title, their status but in life values. And your values are impressive and I feel proud of my choice to know you better.
>**Me:** I really enjoy our conversations and getting to know you

better. You are very easy to talk to.

Erick: Are you mad at me? I have not receive any text from you and you did not answer my questions.

Me: It seems the texts I sent you did not go through and I did not receive your texts either.

Erick: Do you like to go to the movies? Are you romantic? Do you like to hold hands? Do you like flowers?

Me: All of the above!

Erick: Then I want you to know that you are speaking with a man that enjoys to make my significant half enjoy the things she loves to do. Because I believe that the heart of a woman is like soil, a very productive soil. So whatever you sow on it will give you fruits. If you sow the seed of love, you will reap love in abundance even if you are not worth it. If you sow pain you will reap pain from her. It would give me joy to nurture you to become the woman your father hoped you would be. Because a woman comes from our rib meaning when we love them, then we love ourselves and when we hurt them we hurt ourselves. This is the mindset I impact on my boys and want them to grow up to experience and to adopt that as a way of life if you know what I mean.

Me: That is a good metaphor to instill into your children. Showing respect to a woman and your boys seeing the impact it has on your life shows them how it could have a positive impact on their future relationships.

Erick: Are there any responsibilities you believe to be the sole domain of a man or woman? Why do you believe this? Do you believe Guardian Angels are everywhere?

Me: I am very spiritual like my mother. She believed in god and the spiritual world and as I got older I realized there is a higher being in existence. I know someone is watching over me. I believe my guardian angel stays with me constantly and guides me and steps in when needed. As for responsibilities that are gender oriented, I believe that those lines are blurred because both sexes are capable of performing any responsibility. My father taught me I can do anything I set my mind to regardless that I am a girl. He taught me how to support myself including using tools and doing repairs.

Erick: There are millions of people here on earth, you cannot know or meet them all. But there are those who are destined to guide you through every phase of your life as you evolve into a full live human. So these angels come to guide you by waking you up to negative circumstances and come to guide you through positive phases and circumstances. We as humans, we need light and darkness to function fully like electricity.

Me: Recently I lost my aunt she was one of my favorite people on earth. I was named after her we were very close. As she was dying I went for a visit to see her. I wanted to say my goodbye while she was alive. Before I left her last words to me was Keep In Touch! I was shaken because she knew she was dying but still wanted that connection we had to stay in place. She passed away the next morning after I left. I was heartbroken but I know she watches over me now.

Erick: Our duty is to the ambassadors of the will of our creator here on earth and his will is that everyone should live in love, peace, forgiveness, abundance, happiness , joy, affection and sympathy. I love speaking naked to my creator. You know that we were born naked and naked we will leave this earth.

Me: When I spent the last few days with my Aunt, I slept in the bedroom next to her and would sit up late alone with her. She was talking and most assumed it was the medication the caused it but I know she was having conversations with those she loved.

Erick: You came from nothing and you will die with nothing. Everything we need is here on earth, we only take the conscious of how we use those things and the fruits of the consequences. This is my core living value.

Me: We should tell our love ones we love them every time we part, because tomorrow is not guaranteed.

Erick: I want you to know I will adopt it!

(A picture was sent of a brown French Bulldog.)

Erick: Meet Zeus!

(I thought it very odd that a dog with a pink collar was named Zeus, but I try not to be judgmental of another person's pet. Especially when we were in the "getting to know one another" stage.)

Me: I have 2 cats but love dogs too. I like to travel and live alone so cats fit my lifestyle right now.
Erick: Are they friendly?
Me: Cats are different but each animal has their own specific personality. Dogs require more attention than cats do. But they are friendly once they get use to others.

(I sent him pictures of my cats.)

Me: This is Maya and Callie!
Erick: How did you choose their names?
Me: Maya is named after my niece and Callie because she is a Calico breed Cat.
Erick: How are they? How long have you had them?
Me: They are 5 years old in July and I have had them since they were 7 weeks old, they are sisters.
Erick: Do you like to go to the Zoo? Or Animal Reserves?
Me: I love Zoos and Petty Farms but have never been to a Animal Reserve.
Erick: Do you have a bucket list?
Me: Yes, I have a list of things I would love to accomplish before I leave this earth. Doesn't everyone? Do you like to horseback ride?
Erick: Yes, I do. How tall are you? I am 5'11"
Me: I am 5'2" but like tall men. My former husband was 6'1".

> **Erick:** I am happy to hear that! Do you know your blood group?
> **Me:** I am A positive. Most of my siblings are the same. What is your blood type?
> **Erick:** I am type O, honey.

I assumed all they questions were out of curiosity and getting to know one another, but I have since found out they ask you personal questions to use to get to know you so they can keep notes on you. During several conversations, he did respond "noted!" Most times they have several clients, as we victims are called, so they need to keep us on the hook by stringing us along. Also, some feel that the personal info we provide may be clues to passwords they may need to hack. As you can notice, we never stayed on the same subject. The questions seem to bounce around from subject to subject.

> **Erick:** Good Morning, Lady! I was waking up with sweet expectations to connect more to your sweet soul. I hope you slept peacefully?
> **Me:** Yes, I slept peacefully.
> **Erick:** I felt like I found a friendly home for my soul in your world!
> **Me:** I enjoy talking with you. You are easy to talk to.
> **Erick:** Yes, I enjoyed every second of our talks. I feel at peace with you too. The sun is always a sign of good things to come. I hope you know that!
> **Me:** I love the sun even on a cold frigid day, it makes your mood brighter.
> **Erick:** Hahaha! What is your favorite season?
> **Me:** I am a Spring/Summer girl! I hate Fall/Winter. I enjoy the world coming back to life versus dying and hibernation of Fall and Winter.
> **Erick:** You are like me! I love summer but the boys like winter like their mother. Hahaha What's your morning routine?
> **Me:** Always a cup of coffee and watching the news to keep

up on the local news and weather.

Erick: Ok, you have a good reason to do that, it shows that you are a well organized woman.

Me: I live in a rural township and I need to know the road conditions before I travel. What is On your bucket list? Care to share?

Erick: That's very smart of you. Yes, of course! I want to complete my book before I am 65, go tandem Skydiving, Build a holiday home from scratch in a joint location with my significant soulmate. Then become a global citizen by owning an apartment in the world ship. Have you heard of Global Citizenship? Does my bucket list surprise you?

Me: No, not really it seems to fit you. I have not heard of Global Citizenship though.

Erick: Alright, I am glad that is proof we are on the same page. I will tell you more about Global Citizenship.

(Another picture came through of a selfie of him dressed in a casual suit and jeans.)

Erick: Hi Beautiful, I would also love to see some of your photos. Do you have any historical Photos? Here is a website aboardtheworld.com its about universal citizenship. Take your time when you are free to look it up. Okay?

Me: I will check out the website it sounds interesting.

Erick: Do you like fruits? When I was coming to the states my mom gave me a gift and the first was a bible and she wrote in it "The grace to reach any heights in you life is in you"

Me: That is a beautiful verse! What a wonderful mother you have.

Erick: I found this on a day I was devastated after a huge disappointment and I was waiting on the lord and after reading in the bible on a chapter of Peter and I found her verse and that changed my life. Have you ever heard of Viber?

15

Dorothy Harding

Up until this point, we had been conversing on direct messages on our personal phones and the message service on the dating app. It is my understanding now that this is a known scammer technique is to move the "client," as we are referred to, to a non-VOIP, "Voice Over Internet Protocol, as soon as possible. These numbers are impossible to trace unless you are in law enforcement. But during our relationship, we moved quite frequently between different apps and private phone messages.

> **Me:** I never heard of Viber is it a app?
> **Erick:** You go to your App Store and download it, Let me know when you set it up. I was at work and I downloaded the app on my phone. Due to slow Wi-Fi, it took about an hour to do so.
> **Me:** Hello
> **Erick:** Your beautiful! Your profile picture just put a smile on my face.
> **Me:** I took the picture a week ago. I like you call yourself Happy Soul on your profile.

(I was unaware he had already had a Viber account, and being a businessman, I did not question it.)

> **Erick:** What are you doing honey
> **Me:** I am at work taking a break
> **Erick:** Is it night already? I am at home relaxing now and checking up on Mom. I am on Eastern Standard Time zone and she is supposing on Pacific Time zone so we are at a 3 hour difference. (He never mentioned time or day or night. I assumed when he said good morning, he was home or heading to his office or leaving his office was nighttime because he stated he worked late.)
> **Me:** You are a good son.
> **Erick:** My father-in-law often visits my mother. They stay in contact since my late wife passed. My brother lives and works in NY as a life coach and sometimes for me and with me In Vegas she is alone in Bahamas.

(A series of ten family photos came across the app.)

> **Me:** Nice family!
> **Erick:** Do you know your bra size?
> **Me:** Yes, why?
> **Erick:** What is your shoe size?
> **Me:** I wear a size 7 why?
> **Erick:** Noted, what is your favorite collection in your wardrobe?

(Another picture arrived one of his dog Zeus and his leg.)

> **Me:** Nice legs and cute dog.
> **Erick:** When you disagree with your partner do you tend to fight or withdraw?
> **Me:** I try and avoid confrontations. I have to be pushed to fight. My mother once described me as sweetest, kindness person but when cornered will fight back.
> **Erick:** That's wisest way to handle situations. Have you ever physically fought with a man before?
> **Me:** No, not a grown man but with my 3 brothers I have fought. I am the passive type but I am my fathers daughter and can drive a tractor and shoot a gun. My father taught me to never throw the first punch but to defend myself by any means necessary.
> **Erick:** That's absolutely understandable. Why is it that ladies cannot stay without fighting one another?
> **Me:** Jealousy is number one fight among women. Clashing of personalities is another reason and competition is another.
> **Erick:** Did you all sleep in the same room?
> **Me:** No, I shared a room with my sister but we had a huge bedroom the biggest in the house so we had plenty of space.
> **Erick:** Were you naughty growing up?
> **Me:** I was a smart intelligent child who was always curious.

It was my curiosity that seem to get me into trouble.

Erick: The first naughty thing I did that I remember was I was 11 and on Christmas day my father the preacher and sent me to go invite his friend over to the house and it was quite a distance from our home and my mom was preparing a goat meat stew which I loved so much. So I felt my father was taking advantage of me so I walked half way to his friends house and I stood in the shade by the wayside wasting time and as I was sitting there his friend walked passed me and saw me. He asked what I was doing there? I told him I was waiting on a friend and you can imagine when I got home and the man was there and I was embarrassed and did not know what to do. And as a result my dad punished me by ordering my mom not to serve me my meal with the goat meat stew. I was put to bed without a meal.

Me: That is a sweet story.

Erick: Hahaha, you think?

Me: You were mischievous not mean.

Erick: Hahaha, my mom said the same thing.

Me: Did you ever tell your boys this story?

Erick: Yes I did and guess what they said? That I am the naughtiest dad in the world! Can you Imagine! Who is naughty me or them?

Me: you know they are going to throw that story up every time you discipline them when they are naughty.

Erick: I have proper communication with them soul to soul and man to man kind of relationship with them.

Me: That means you are a wonderful father to take time to spend with your sons and nourish them.

Erick: My mother had a still birth, she was supposed to be my elder sister.

Me: Wow, that's awful! I came from such a huge family and my mother was one of 2 sets of twins.

Erick: Do you think you would have had twins at one point in your life?

Me: I never really thought about it but one of my Uncles who was a twin had a set of twins. and his twin brothers granddaughter had a set of twins. I was diagnosed with cervical cancer in my mid twenties and battled for several years and ended up having a procedure that rendered me sterile to kill the cancer so I was told I would never bear a child.
Erick: Praise god you are here for me to encounter! Do you still have the scars from the surgeries?
Me: My mother told me god had other plans for me here on earth. I have some external scars but I have internal scarring and I carried the emotional scars too. I did not feel a reason to marry afterwards I knew I would remain single.
Erick: Amen, you have a inspirational spirit. You are sent for your generation for a purpose.
 Do you eat garlic?
Me: I love spicy foods but not heat. I love garlic but cooked not raw. I eat a lot of fish and chicken and stay clear of pork and keep red meat to a minimum. I love fresh salads and fruits mostly whole foods not processed.
Erick: What is your idea of fair division of labor in the household?
Me: Are you asking about the work load inside the home or outside?

He ignored my respond and did not answer; instead, he continued to ask more questions. I always questioned why did he not answer, but I think I overwhelmed him with answering with indirect questions versus just answering his question. I am not a submissive type of woman.

Erick: Do you consider yourself an easygoing person or are you comfortable with a firm plan of action?
Me: I am only indecisive when it comes to shopping otherwise I think things over and make a decision based on fact. I tend to compromise more than most but am generally happy with with most decisions I make.

Dorothy Harding

Erick: That shows you stay very optimistic, am I right?
Me: I was born optimistic despite the pitfalls life throws my way.
Erick: That is what attracts me more and more to you, My darling! Do you like to be freshly? Showered and wear clean clothes everyday even on weekends and especially on Vacations?

Me: Yes, I am a very clean person! I bathe daily and put on clean clothes daily. Sometimes I bathe and change clothes more than once a day especially on vacation.
Erick: What is your idea of perfect relaxation?
Me: I love a cold drink and just chill on a beach all day long!
Erick: Something like this?

(He sent me several pictures of him lounging on beaches in chairs.)

Me: Your my kind of man!
Erick: I have been looking for you and now that I have found you I want to be with you for the rest of my living here on earth.
Me: You are a sweetheart!
Erick: What do you do when you get really angry?
Me: I try not to get angry if someone is provoking me I usually back away and won't engage. I have to be pushed to engage. I use my head before emotions. My mother had a saying What comes around goes around and that is generally true.

Erick: That is the best way to handle such. I do the same. What brings you most joy?
Me: Surround yourself with the people who make you the most happiest. Laughter is the best medicine. Joy comes from spending quality time with those you love the most.

Erick: You are like me, my core value is live, love, laugh and life. What makes you most Insecure? How so you handle your insecurities?

Me: I so not get insecure! I do not get jealous either. Most people with bad intentions Actually get nervous around me because I cannot be intimidated. My ex-husband had a lot of insecurities it plagued our marriage but even he knew I could not be intimidated because I was secure on who I was. I got rid of any lingering insecurities in my young adult life. I do not play games, I hate games but if forced to play I will win. My ex figured this out and hated it, because he liked games.

Erick: I am not surprised you overcame because you are a born fighter and that is your testimony and you are to use your experience to impact your world now. Honey, I really enjoyed our chat but I am falling asleep now.

Me: Sweet Dreams

Erick: I hope we can continue building on this wonderful bond we are developing?

Me: I am willing to continue if you are willing.

Erick: You are the soul I seek out to find at my age. I know what I want and what and what I am looking for and when I find what I am looking for I go for it with everything within me. If I win I celebrate my success, if I lose I learn that its not the way to go about it then I re-strategize.

At this time, there were unanswered questions I had. But not enough to tip me off that I was talking to someone who was manipulating me into believing he was who he said he was. If he had presented himself as an American or in the military I would have known. I am from a military family, parent, siblings, etc. Plus, I spent ten years working with military active duty and retirees; I am used to them and their policies. He knew I was connected to military. It would be stupid for him to portray himself as one. Scammers use military, oil rig workers, and traveling businessmen as occupations.

Erick: Good Morning beautiful soul, how did you sleep? I just got home from the gym what are you doing?
Me: Just drinking my coffee and staying warm it is cold here.
Erick: How do you like your coffee, my sweet?
Me: Just cream, I cut back on sugar usage. How do you drink yours?
Erick: I am more of a herbal tea person, I drink lots of green tea.
Me: I like green tea especially with honey to cut the bitterness.
Erick: Do you drink alcohol?
Me: I like a glass of wine on occasion mostly Italian white wines and some reds.
Erick: That sweet my love, I love both too. Have you ever been to a wine tasting?
Me: Yes, I have I have been to quite a few in Northern Michigan there are quite a few wineries I have been to. There is estimated 30 wineries in one area alone. Have you been to one?
Erick: I have been to a couple of wine tastings also. What is your plan for the day?
Me: I have some projects to complete and work to do around the house. What are your plans?
Erick: I am home precious but I am leaving for the office soon. I have meetings with some of my staff.
Me: Let me know when you want to video chat, Erick.
Erick: Yes, most definitely, thank you my heart keeper. Are you still on Zoosk?
Me: I disabled my account. You were my last chance at online dating so I disabled my account. I have no interest to look any further.
Erick: Wow really! This is not a joke? I disabled my account also, when did you disable yours?
Me: Yesterday, I disabled it.

Later I realized he never disabled the account; in fact, that's how he met other women. I know there were two other women or more whom he was scamming, and one of them told me she met him on Zoosk dating website! A YouTube video "To Love Somebody" by Michael Bolton was texted to me.

Me: I love that song!
Erick: Did you ever catch any of your parents doing naughty things?
Me: No, my parents were very conservative. They kept their time together private.
Erick: I had funny experiences with electronics!
Me: What funny experiences did you have with electronics?
Erick: I was curious to know how they function and then I would unscrew the radio or the device I was interested in then I would find it difficult to screw it back in perfectly and it ended up being a problem with my dad. I tried carpentry with my dad because he was handy with that but most of my interest was in electronics. Have you done anything sexual naughty before?
Me: Yes, what about you?
Erick: I had a very naughty encounter when I was 22 years old. I went to a club in my country where lots of tourist come to party when they visit Nassau. I met these 2 beautiful ladies dancing together and kissing each other honey and that was my first time to see such a thing and I was amused and went up to them and told them how amazing they were and how turned on I was watching them together. They asked me if I would love to watch them play with their bodies and they would pay me for the pleasure which was unbelievable. So I followed them to their hotel room and saw my first live porn. They paid me $2100 but they never allowed me to touch them. I had to masturbate in their presence!
Me: Wow, did that happen in your country often?
Erick: No, not to me. Honey can we have a video call before I leave the office?
Me: Sure we can video chat whenever you are ready!
Erick: What are you doing, my darling?
Me: I am at work doing some paperwork at my desk.

> **Erick:** I know everything you touch is always a success. I am excited and nervous all at the same time, Donna.
> **Me:** I feel the same way, Erick.
> **Erick:** Would you consider moving in with your new man, beautiful?
> **Me:** I would consider it in due time. I put your picture on my phone as my screen saver.
> **Erick:** Wow, This is way more than a sign for me. I will do my best to walk you through a path least expected. What is your ideal Friday night?
> **Me:** I usually work on Friday nights unless I am off so I spend them planning my weekend.
> **Erick:** What is your typical weekend?
> **Me:** Usually cleaning and running errands sometimes me time or time with my sister or brother.
> **Erick:** I always have proper time to enjoy a conversation with mom and sometimes the boys the boys come over with me and we go shopping or they suggest something else we can go and do.

I received an incoming video call. He had just arrived home, and it entailed him walking and talking, and the dog in the pictures he sent was greeting him. There was no face-to-face chat. It lasted about five minutes. I realize now, talking with other victims, there is no face-to-face video chat. They have technology to fake videos, so you see someone whose videos they stole and use their own voices. Also, a lot of times during our relationship, he mentioned calling his mother, and I, knowing now he had several other women on the hook, realized there was no mother; he had to spend time speaking with the other victims too.

> **Erick:** You are a beautiful woman and I felt very nervous for a minute.
> **Me:** I loved seeing your precious dog and hearing your voice.
> **Erick:** Aww, my precious! I have made the right choice in you and I can see myself becoming
>   a new man with you.

Me: I think we would be better individuals together than apart, Eric, Don't you agree?

Erick: Yes, you have completed the statement from my soul that is carved on the same path I designed for me. You are beautiful and have a peaceful aura and a beautiful voice. I hope my tired nature did not disappoint you, Honey.

Me: Not at all, Erick. I loved hearing your voice!

Erick: And I could see my soulmate, my companion. You are patient with me because your soul has also found a friend in me. I will be driving home shortly, Donna. I want you to know that I set out to find someone who is really ready to welcome a new soul into their world and begin A new chapter together to fulfill one another expectation of enjoying love from the opposite sex and a friend for my heart. I feel so much at peace.

Me: Are you home yet?

Erick: Yes, beautiful! I wish I could come back home to my friend always. You know what I mean?

Me: Yes, I do!

Erick: Did you ever welcome your exes home when they would go out? How did you welcome them home?

Me: Yes, I always welcomed my significant other home and always with a warm hug and kisses.

Erick: I know that feeling and miss that feeling. Sometimes my late wife would drive to the office for quick sex. Have you ever done such a thing before?

Me: That is a wonderful woman and no I have not. My husband was a diesel mechanic and when
 I did visit him at work he was covered in heavy black grease he had to take a shower and
 change before he came home or as soon as he arrived home. Besides he was always surrounded
 by co-workers he was the shift boss.

Erick: I can see from the picture you sent me he was a big man. How did you meet?

Me: Both of our sisters worked together and they set us up

> on a blind date. What about your late wife how did you meet?
> **Erick:** I will call and tell you better, OK?

I noticed he never answered my questions when they pertained to his family members. If he was operating from a script, it would make sense, because he had no planned answers for the unexpected questions I asked him. It is well known that romance scammers usually work with a planned script and take notes to keep track of what they have said to you or what information you have provided. On scammer websites and Facebook pages, they buy and sell such scripts to use on their "clients," as we are referred to as.

> **Erick:** What is your greatest strength, honey?
> **Me:** Patience and Loyalty are my best strengths.
> **Erick:** Did I tell you I am writing a book on patience?
> **Me:** Yes, you mentioned that.
> **Erick:** You know the first encounter that brought my consciousness to that revelation?
> **Me:** No, but please continue.
> **Erick:** The law of nature is just for you to grow and you must be conceived and you must be nurtured in the womb for 9 months before you can be born. If you are born before the 9 months then you are a premature seed and there is no guarantee you will survive the challenges of childhood growth. this is the same with the rules of life. Even when the doctors told us my late wife could not bear fruits, I refused to accept their report rather I told her that as long as we sleep in the same bed and keep enjoying sex and love making together that I will sow the seed of wonderful kids in her womb and she agreed with me. With her whole faith she called me her captain and I would put my hand on her womb and speak words of life to her womb and telling her womb that I saw a productive soil in her world and I want my fruits given to me. Miraculously, she took it in and gave birth to our first child. I thought that there is a time and season for everyone and everything and you must wait for your season. The waiting

process builds you and nurtures you. Your creator expects you to trust in him so he knows what is good for you not otherwise. And enjoy your waiting season to grow patience. #live#love#laugh#life.

Me: That is a beautiful story, Erick. I love the way that you think.

Erick: So I want to dedicate the remaining years with my soulmate. Living out in love and also impacting our world with peace, love, laughter and forgiveness because we are human and we are bound to make mistakes so we have to decide to forgive each other even before we oath our commitment to entrusting each others heart and trust in each others world. Knowing that destiny out our paths to impact on each other so that we will fulfill our calling here on earth. Do you know why we are called?

Me: It is Gods will when and why we are called, only heaven can answer that question. Forgiveness feeds the soul and makes us better people. I do know that people are placed in our lives for a reason. It is up to us to find out what that purpose will serve in our life. I know our souls have met for a reason.

Erick: That is the womb that births true love, I hope you know what I mean Donna.

Me: I love your prospective on life, you have a beautiful soul, Mr. Andersen.

Erick: I am flattered, Honey. You are a light also. I went to a prayer and fasting church back home before locating to the states and then a prophet of god told me that I'm chosen to be a servant of god to take the knowledge and glory of God and calling upon my late dad globally.

Glory be to my creator I tried my best to run away from this calling upon my life but so many circumstances and grace kept bringing me back to the path. So I choose to accept the call and told the creator if he can bless me with wealth, health and my destined soulmate and best friend in a woman and bless me with beautiful kids, I will dedicate everyday of my living to bring every living soul to the consciousness of his love regardless of our weaknesses. So when I lost my late wife I never gave up the faith that I will end my journey with my soulmate and best friend by my side and my faith. And I pray and ask god for my needs and he meets them. And that's my confidence and more reason and proof that he will send the right woman in my path. So my book will also be a platform that I am using to share my journey with my creator through patience and trusting completely in him. Now I am in the next phase of my life where I am completely ready to embark on a new chapter of enjoying everyday doing and involving in things that makes us happy and bringing out the best of each other to seed into our children to our third and forth generations.

> **Me:** When I was going through my divorce and I moved away but the pain I felt moved with me. I realized you have to deal with head on, there is no running away from it. Every single night I cried for the pain to stop. I was on my hands and knees begging god to ease this pain in my heart and soul. One day I awoke and the pain stopped. I just needed to bring god back into my life to help me deal with a really tough time in my life. So in my life he will remain! You see people will come and go in your life but god is always there consistently for you when you believe in him. I know I will endure more pain in life and I know who to turn to for guidance to overcome that pain.
>
> **Erick:** Now your soil is ready to be cultivated again with the seed of true and practical love because that's the way to reap the fruits of love, peace, laughter, affection, emotions and great favor that comes from your world. I have found a home in your soul, my precious.
>
> **Me:** Baby, I just go home from work can you give me a few minutes Ok?

(I tried to call him several times, and the phone just rang and rang and no answer; it was several hours later before he responded, and it was through text. I texted him, Are you sleeping?)

Erick: Hi Beautiful, I know you must of heard this a million times before. Its amazing how you Let me into your life, I am so glad that when I knocked on the door to your world that you opened it and let me in and this is my assurance to you that I will swim the deepest seas with you and climb the highest mountains with you. Just believe I will not let you go, because with you is where I'd rather be. So I'm imploring you to take my hands and confide in me because I've made the choice to build up the best of you. For you to share with me and the world around you that god has sent us to be his ambassadors of love, peace and happiness and laughter, forgiveness and living to sell the will of our creator to manifest around us which comes with agape love as a result.
Me: That is beautiful, Erick! I love the way you think. I think it is a blessing we met.
Erick: That is how I feel beautiful! I just wanted to share that with you before I close my eyes my Darling. I promise you my eternal love as long as I live. I will also dedicate to making the best version of you and guiding you to your full glow because you are my gift from destiny. now lets rest our soul in the hands of our creator and sleep with peace ready for the journey ahead my rib.
Me: Amen

Six hours later, I received a video call, but I was sound asleep. I tried to return the call but no answer, so I sent a text: "Sorry I missed your call but I did not hear my phone."

Erick: I can already feel your presence. I know we are not perfect nor to I expect perfection from you and I do not want you to expect perfection from me but I want you to believe in commitment and I am promising you my commitment in making everyday of your life with me and I hope you will consider the best years of your living and experiencing the power of agape love from a man here on earth. Lets then commit to our future boldly and enjoy the journey.

(I received a video call from Erick it lasted about five minutes.)

Erick: I just wanted to hear your beautiful voice, Donna. How is your day so far?

(Was basically the conversation during the brief video chat. Still no face-to-face chat.)

Erick: If you decide you can have love, time with family, lots of money and a relationship with god all at the same time. They are all not mutually exclusive and lack of time is not a excuse. We have four areas of our life. The staff, The professional, The spiritual and the economic. Each one has a purpose and should have a equal priority in your life. Personally my purpose is that my children be happy and have a home full of love. In the professional, it is to impact the lives of many people and do something big. In the spiritual, it is to maintain faith and a relationship with god. In the economic, to create and attract abundance and mass prosperity. Work and build your four areas of life and it guarantees that you can live a full and prosperous life. This is how I feel.
Me: That is a smart plan. You must have put a lot of thought into this design for your life.
Erick: Yes, and I have found you to be my completeness. I cannot wait to show you off to my watchers. To show them how proud and happy and I am energized for this journey of happiness. What a beautiful way to end my life. Truth be told it is no longer a dream but a reality. I just want to thank you for being a part of my story.
Me: Thank you, Erick! That is beautiful and thank you for entering my life when I really needed you the most.
Erick: And I want you to know that from today you are the

best. Everyday can be a excellent day. Every weekend is excellent because we decided to be together. Now that my children are growing, I am at a stage in life of keeping the family together. Do you know when a man throws in the towel? When the family is not enough reason to be ambitious, move forward and accumulate money? I will explain, when a man is limited he lacks money and say "Money and things are not important only family and happiness is" This is the worst thing you can think and do for your family. Money is the number one tool to keep the family together.

I did not say Happy that's another theme. When Mark and Logan was born, I knew I had to achieve success somehow. It's the reason why when we fall we keep on fighting.

Do you know how many families have separated because the father and mother passed?

Away or leave their country for another country in many cases, in search for a pinch job.

How many children in my country after growing up and borrowing to study in college then go away from home. From the family for a fucking job! Young people who leave and then the parents only see them once a year. Is that living happy? Money is used to help children undertake their future and several projects because they fail several times to try and it can affect you financially. Money is used to buy them like a house so that 50% of their income from a pinch job will not be able to pay the rent and keep them limited. Understand this the money you have worked and managed to accumulate is to ensure your future.

It is a powerful tool, use it. If you are not happy and you have no money is another topic then you screwed up as a father then. Imagine my children are limited and possibly suffering because I made the wrong decision. What do you think, Donna?

I believe this statement is his belief as to why he is scamming women out of hundreds and thousands of dollars. I think he truly believes that scamming women out of their hard-earned money is justified so he can have money to take care of his family properly! At the time, I found this statement strange because even though I have never been to The Bahamas, I thought it was economically in better shape than most Caribbean Islands. I have been to most of the Caribbean Islands and have witnessed how they live. I know tourism plays a large part, but The Bahamas is in a better position economically to prosper. But I truly do believe he thinks money equals happiness and likes to impress others with his wealth. This is my opinion! Form your own as you read along on his words.

> **Me:** Wow, that is a powerful insight into life. I can only speak for myself and through my own upbringing. But money can be the root of all evil and it does not guarantee love or happiness,
> **Erick:** This I do know. You can have all the money in the world but it can not buy you happiness, peace or health. That must come from your soul within.
> **Erick:** Hello beautiful! My precious something heavenly happened today.
> **Me:** Tell me about your day you seem excited.
> **Erick:** I did not drive to do my shopping and the cab driver and I began a conversation he was an elderly man. We talked about religion and he began to express the actions of those he was dealing with while he was a religious worshiper of God. He spoke about the gossiping backbiting and jealousy. As we were discussing this I was led in my spirit to bring him to the right knowledge of God's plan for his creation. I asked him to join me for lunch and then we spoke more deeply. I begun to open the eyes of his spirit to the finished work of grace and then he told me since he was born he had never had the gospel in this manner. God led me to him honey and I prayed with him and then when I got home I had to prepare for a late invitation to an associates marriage anniversary.

First, I was startled by the fact he lives in Boulder City, Nevada, and had sent me numerous pictures of several vehicles and was taking a cab to get toiletries at a store! It confused me a bit because I Googled the area, and it seemed he lived in a subdivision in town. Cab versus Uber or Lyft driver was another red flag. Obviously, he was not where he said he was, but it left a question in my mind as to why have a driver take you a short distance for toiletries. I rationalized it by thinking he was Bahamian and maybe that was his culture. Obviously, he was somewhere else, or the story was completely scripted.

Me: You have a beautiful soul and that was a nice gesture to help him to see the light to god.
Erick: I am humbled to be a vessel for destiny to unveil ignorance from a generation. Do you believe that marriages are stronger if a woman defers to her husband in most areas? Do you feel either in control or taken care of?
Me: I believe marriages are only stronger if each allows the other to strengthen the others weaknesses. I do not believe anyone would be happy in a marriage where they are being controlled. I believe in mutual alliances to achieve common goals because that makes a happy and healthy marriage. If you attempt to control another in a marriage you are doomed to fail and happiness and resentment sets in. Defer to one another desires and needs will only strengthen a marriage.
Erick: Honey I believe in equality, I am not selfish and I don't like it. I believe whatever I put into you, I am getting back regardless. If I sow seed of love and peace into your life. I know for a fact I am getting it back. As I am growing in every aspect of my life, I want to grow with you, mentally, physically, financially, sexually and spiritually. So together we can come and testify to the fact that life is good if you understand it. Our life will be a channel of hope to those who does not know the left from the right. I love the fact that we are on the same page. You know what I mean right?
Me: Yes, Erick I understand everything your saying. I think God put us on this earth to meet certain people that will have an impact on our lives. I believe it was meant for us to meet. I believe each of us were put on earth for a purpose and others you meet in your lifetime was destined to serve a pur-

pose in one another lives. And some is to learn a lesson in life. I like that you seem to be a kind and passionate man. You seem to have patience which is one of my favorite virtues. I am beginning to admire you as a person and a man for those reasons.

Erick: That's what happens when the lines begin to fall in pleasant places precious. What did you learn about race and ethnic differences as a child?

Me: I grew up in Detroit and learned about race issues early in life. I lived in Detroit during the riots in 1967. I attended a predominately black elementary school and had black and white teachers. my early childhood was tainted with war and racial equality. I was taught to treat all people as I wish to be treated and that has never changed throughout my life. I find different cultures and customs interesting and you never stop learning from one another. I can honestly say I have met a lot of different cultures in Detroit it became a melting pot of different religions and races and that is what makes America evolve. Racism is taught not embedded in your DNA and if we listen to children they automatically accept others as they are with curiosity not hate. We did move toward the end of the riots we could not attend school because of the violence and no child should be raised in violence ever. As a woman I am a minority and I have been discriminated against so I feel for those who are not appreciated for who they are as a individual versus the color of their skin. In Gods eyes we are all created equal and I hold the same stance.

Erick: This life is so beautiful once you begin to understanding the root of creation. Then you begin to live out each day with revelation of doing the will of God here on earth. I strongly believe that your first responsibility entrusted to you by our creator is to be a man to the world around you , then secondly to be a husband to a wife, that's your own rib. Your completeness and her completeness then you seek out this understanding to find a woman who is your destiny. When you find her with revelation, then you both come together to fulfill the purpose of creation then to our children who will become our utmost responsibility. This is entrusted upon us by our creator of life. We have a responsibility to harness our children. Your ideals and and their talents and their gifts and to set them free to shine and illuminate their world with talents, gifts and ideals through the revelations that you will bring them the key. The creator has entrusted to me and you to come together to become parents and partners in union for each other to love.

Me: That is a beautiful path to look forward to, Mr. Andersen.

Erick: When I come to a new path that I want to embark upon you know what I would do and advise you to do? You have to look at yourself in the mirror and get a piece of paper and put it next to you. Then write down everything you wished you would have done better and regretted not doing then burn that list and put it behind you. Then you write down everything you want to be doing now to keep your heart happy. Place your list by the mirror and promise yourself to begin to achieve those things daily. This should be your new choice of living.

Me: I think I have always been an optimistic person one who wakes up each day feeling it's a new start to make it better than the day before. I refuse to live in the past and always learn from my mistakes. If you look back it not to look at the bad but the good memories otherwise you do not learn the lessons life has to teach you. Mistakes can be used to make you a stronger person not to hold on for resentment. Choose your words wisely if you speak unkindly to another you cannot take those words back as my mother would say think before you speak. It does not make you a better person to hurt another intentionally it makes you weaker. A stronger person is one who admits their faults and asks for forgiveness. Letting go of the past allows you to grow as a person and put your best foot forward for the future.

Erick: Yes you have to see your weaknesses and accept them because the consequences of the fruits of our ignorance is enough to attract the wrong paths to us. We have the same 24 hours in the everyday its what you do with your time that defines your eternity and your choice through life either to enjoy everyday as if it was your last. When your spirit leaves your body with the right mindset. There is 52 weeks in the year and my priority is to make them memorable with the people destiny brings me in contact with. I have beautiful memories with my kids and deceased wife now I want to enjoy it with my significant other half because that is the age I am at now. To embark on this new phase I need my soulmate by my side and I hope you know what I mean, Honey. My full name is ARW Erick Andersen, what is your full name?

Me: My full name is Donna Jo Harding

Erick: Those are beautiful names honey. What do you think of change of names?

Me: I believe once you are married you should take your husbands last name as your surname. Otherwise I don't see a reason for a name change unless your parents gave you a hideous first name that you simply cannot live with. What does the ARW before your first name mean? What does it represent in your culture?

Erick: It is to identify me as a decedent of an island of the Atlantic Ocean east of Florida and Cuba. Do you understand what your name means? How is a part of your destiny?

Me: I was suppose to be a boy after 3 girls my father wanted a boy so my name was suppose to be Joseph after my Great-Grandfather. But I came out a girl and I was named after my Aunt Donna. And I have Jo as a middle name. My mother believed all children were gifts from God she cherished each and everyone of us.

Erick: You are really an interesting soul, honey. Your name is a confirmation that you are destined to be a gift of your generation and any man that grabs this reality will get the full package of the gifts you carry. How do you describe your current state of health?

Me: I am in good health, I take care of myself and go for regular check-ups. I believe it is your job to do your very best to sustain a healthy lifestyle. That is Gods intention for you to take good care of the body he gifted you. I am not saying I have not had my fair share of health issues but that is even more reason to take care of it. You only receive one physical body on this planet and its your job to take care of it.

Erick: Do you believe it is a sacred responsibility to take care of yourself? Do you believe that taking care of your physical and mental health is part of honoring your marriage vows?

Me: Yes, you should never let your health go mental or physical but not for a marriage but for your soul. God gave you life and it is your job to sustain it and make the right decisions. God sometimes throws us issues to see how we will handle the situation regarding our wellbeing. It makes a good marriage to both be on the same page regarding maintaining a healthy lifestyle.

Erick: I am glad you feel this way, Donna. You owe it to yourself to speak perfect health to yourself when you pray for your soul. Knowing when the creator created you he made you in perfect health. Are there any Genetic diseases in your family or history of cancer?

Me: There are cancer and heart disease that runs rampant in my immediate family. I was diagnosed with cervical cancer when I was in my mid 20's and have beat it. I have a very healthy heart. I also have Hypothyroidism and will take medication the rest of my life. other than that I am very healthy. I want to live my best life and that requires taking good care of yourself and living a healthy lifestyle.

Erick: The power of life and death is in your words, do you know what that means?

Me: Yes, I do!

Erick: Then you should know that the end of such affliction has come that's why you have Also received the revelation of the world. Do you have Health Insurance? Dental Insurance? Do you believe in joint family medical plans?

Me: Yes, I do I have medical, dental and vision insurances and believe the whole family should also be insured. When I was married we had joint health insurance coverage. I also believe in preventative maintenance which is cover with most plans. Yearly physical exams and testing to keep your health in working order. You must do this to prevent disease and extend your quality of life. Erick, I am leaving my sisters house and will be on the road for several hours can you call me or we can text later?

Erick: my precious, the sign you need to know that when the right man comes into your life when everything that is not functioning, spiritually, mentally, physically, financially, emotionally and environmentally will cause you to begin to glow and look younger. That is why I call aging with grace with your soulmate, your completeness by your side together fulfilling the purpose of your existence here on earth. Not just as ordinary beings but your duty as a soul in the body of a woman is to be a vessel of honor. A woman of virtue, a woman who understands her responsibilities as a female creature, as a wife, as a partner, as a friend, as a womb bearer, as a rib to her man and as a keeper and bearer of generations then she will leave the face of this earth with angels who will welcome her soul and spirit when she departs this earth. Declaring to the giver of life and to the angels how great he is to be gifted with her life and also her children and her children's children and that they will testify that they are all a product of a great woman's virtue and that's how you should depart this world. Would you consider moving in with me?

Me: I would consider it, Erick!

Erick: Amen, I want to finish reading some scripture then we can have a deeper chat, OK? I will share some pictures of my family with you before I close my eyes. I have some training with some senior staff tomorrow and should begin preparing for my trip to New York this week or next. And we also should arrange your coming or me coming to get you soon. Please rest under grace my precious.

I received several various photos of him with his boys and several family members. To date, I have received roughly a thousand or more pictures. I assumed he had these pictures stored on his phone, but now I realized he must have been copying and pasting a lot of these photos he had sent me. Some seemed older; none, until much later in the relationship, were recent, except for his selfies. This caused me no red flags at the time. I did ask at one point, several months prior to finding out that this was all a scam, if the picture he just sent was a recent photo. He seemed caught off guard as to what I meant. That was an unknown red flag because when they scam us, they seem to work on a script or timetable, and I think my questions seemed to throw him off because he would ask me why I asked a certain question.

I received a selfie the next morning; he was in his car behind the wheel.

Erick: Having a presentation and training with my senior staff. I pray for an excellent spirit to accompany you all day.

I received several photos of him in what looked like empty conference room set up for giving a presentation. It also accompanied a short video of him giving a presentation, but the video had no sound. This is typical of a scammer; when the voices do not match, they do voiceovers or no-sound videos to convince you they are who they say they are. I have always believed that through every lie told there is a bit of truth embedded within, but I could not decipher what was real or fake because I didn't know how true to the script he followed.

Erick: Do you know about Lithium?
Me: Are you talking about Lithium Batteries?
Erick: One of the major companies are open to private investors because the demand for production is on the rise so the need for private investors are needed to increase produc-

tion and my company is contracted to bring investors on board.

Me: Wow, that is great!

Erick: This is my website, Honey. www.peakcockbusinessgroup.com so you have the proper ideal of my services. I want you to know everything about me honey because we have decided to build a new path. You are an independent woman and anything that you seek I know that will lead your heart to love me as I am a better man so please feel free.

Me: Thank you for sharing this with me but I am not seeking a man to take care of me but seeking a soulmate to work along side with. Sharing your past helps me to see the future we might have together.

Erick: Awesome, the lines are falling in pleasant places for us that is all I can say. What is your occupation and your line of work? How are you paid hourly or monthly? Do you feel you are paid your net worth?

Me: I work as a military civilian but am under a non-disclosure to discuss my job. I work on government contracts. I am paid bi-monthly and make enough to support myself and provide my needs. I take any job I perform very seriously and give 100 percent to everything I do. I receive a fair pay and receive a bonus and raise yearly based on my performance.

Erick: Who handles the finances in the relationship?

Me: I handle my own finances but when I was married my ex-husband handled the big purchases and I handled the home finances and we discussed everything together. Later I handled most all finances when he became disabled.

Erick: My late wife liked numbers and I enjoyed it when I would get the household budget from her. Do you believe in family budgets?

Me: Of course, in order the meet your mutual goals you must create a budget. I still as a single woman live within a budget. They can help you save for the future and vacations and big purchases.

Erick: Hahaha, I enjoy shopping so we can go shop for clothes together holding hands. I am glad you like to budget it gives the family a financial direction. Do you think individuals within a marriage should have separate bank accounts in addition to joint bank accounts? Do you feel bills should be divided based on percentages of each partners salary?

Me: I am glad you like shopping with your partner, as far as bank accounts me and my ex-husband had a joint account but later he set up a separate account but my name was attached to access in case of emergency. But if you are not married and bring significant property into the marriage it is up to you to decide if you want your partner to have access to that money or property. Keep in mind I have always worked and brought a separate paycheck into our marriage. As far as bills we would pay all bills out of the joint bank account regardless of how much who made what.

Erick: I was raised to understand that my responsibility to be the root and my rib of the tree and together we bring branches so we feed them and we water and weed and harvest our seeds and yes, I believe that two are now one and we become as one. Do you have significant debt, Honey?

Me: I have a small amount because I was on medical leave up until a few months ago, but its nothing I cannot handle and its not significant.

Erick: Do you gamble?

Me: It should be do I like to gamble? I like to have something to show for what I spend but I have gambled but with very small controlled amounts at a Casino with others. I really am the type to spend my money on entertainment versus gambling.

Erick: I believe that two are now one and we become one in union and what is mine is yours to care for and what is yours for me to care for and that we are responsible for each others well being. As you grow I grow and as I grow you grow that way we are yielding harvest and will sustain our generations.

Do you believe a certain amount of money should be set aside for pleasure, even if you are on a tight budget?

Me: Yes, I do because every good marriage needs family or couple time together. When you both work hard you both should enjoy the fruits of your labor and whether it is a weekend getaway or a full fledge vacation it is need to refuel your marriage.

Erick: Have you ever used money in a way of controlling a relationship? Has anyone ever tried to control you with money?

Me: No, because I value people over money. I place a relationship value over money. no one has ever tried to control me with money. I have always had a independent mind and spirit and cannot really be controlled.

Erick: Do you believe in prenuptial agreements? Under what circumstances?

Me: It depends on the couple but if your asking if I would ever sign one the answer is a simple yes. I want to build a life of trust and respect with my partner and I believe what you bring into the relationship is yours if you wish to share it that is totally up to you to decide. A prenuptial is to protect both parties not just one side. I hope that answers your question!

Erick: I want you to share my world and I want you to share yours with me and together we will leave a legacy behind. I know you are the type of woman I can entrust my inheritances with even when I am not there. I am certain that you will use it to set our generations right. Do you have any inheritance or property that you are willing to discuss before moving in with me?

Me: When I went through the divorce several years ago I had to sell most of my property and spent most of my savings. My divorce cost me thousands of dollars so I had to start over from scratch and rebuild my life. So the answer is no to your question.

Erick: So do you have any savings he left you or assets that you have for yourself?

Me: I had a little savings I have accumulated, but I will need it to pay bills before I start anew with you. He sent me several pictures of several cars they look to be Porsche's and a Bentley.

Erick: I love cars! Do you like cars?

Me: Of course I love cars I grew up in Motor City! You would be surprised how much I know about cars!

Erick: Do you like properties?

Me: I do but not the maintenance. That I leave to the man of the house. Those are nice cars you must love expensive white cars.

Erick: Yes, I love cars and fast ones. I love and own properties also.

He sent twenty-seven photos of various scenes of properties and homes it was hard to decipher if it was from the same home or several different homes. Some pictures he was in, and some were of his family, deceased wife and children. Now I realize they were all stolen pictures off of social media; some I found of the man whose photos he stole to use as his own picture, but some could have been stolen from others. I now feel sorry for the other victim because I know his likeness and family photos have been used multiple times to scam victims out of thousands, if not millions, of dollars.

The Facebook page was set up in 2017 until December 2019. But Erick never knew I knew about it. He used the website and dating website to lure me and others.

Erick: I want to share some of my memories with you, Honey.

Me: Wow, those are beautiful photos. I love the palm trees and scenery. I cannot wait to See these in person.

More photos, a compilation of 124 photos was sent, all various family and him and his kids along with the wedding and his deceased wife. Due to the fact I filed a complaint through ic3.gov, the FBI's internet crime division, I was told to hold on to all correspondence between me and him. It is hard looking at these photos now because they were stolen from the other victim to scam me and others. But if it means one day him getting caught, it would be my pleasure to archive this evidence.

> **Me:** Wow, gorgeous photos, Erick!
>
> **Erick:** I have everything I set out as a young man to archive, I was seeking the missing piece of me. When I reached out and found you now I am excited about the next chapter of destiny. I have enjoyed grace.
>
> **Me:** You are truly a wonderful man. I am excited to see where life takes us on this journey.
>
> **Erick:** I love you baby! What are you doing?
>
> **Me:** I love you too, I am sitting here cuddling with my fur babies and dreaming of our future together.
>
> **Erick:** I am also thinking of how I can impact your life to be the best for me. I am excited you can see me in your dreams. I will also teach you all I can, while you teach me also.
>
> **Me:** That is a deal, babe.
>
> **Erick:** Have you ever tried to invest before?
>
> **Me:** I had 401k's and IRA's
>
> **Erick:** Ok, do you have any now?
>
> **Me:** No, I had cashed out them to pay for my divorce.
>
> **Erick:** Ok love, If I offer to teach you investment and guide you would you be interested to learn?
>
> **Me:** I have the ability to learn anything I set my mind to. I would love to learn investments.
>
> **Erick:** Alright my wife then I will personally to guide you because now two good heads are better than one.
>
> **Erick:** From the day that I met you, Donna. I knew that your love would be everything that I ever wanted in my life, From the moment you spoke my name I knew everything had changed. because of you I felt my life would be complete.
>
> **Me:** I feel the same about you too, Erick. When I seen your profile on Zoosk I thought this is a wonderful man.

Erick: Awww, honey what made you feel that way about me, Donna?

Me: By the look in your eyes you know your eyes are the window to our souls don't you?

Erick: That's very true, I want to wake up everyday and call you my baby, I need you for the rest of my life baby girl. I need you by my side and I feel the two of us will make everything missing in our lives and everything when I think of the way my heart feels when we communicate and I accept that I love you and I will never deny that. I need you Donna!

Me: I love you, too Erick

Erick: Mark is creative and Logan is academically excellent.

Me: Do the boys argue a lot or loving and accept one another?

Erick: Initially as kids it was about wanting the same share for everything until I explained to them that they are entitled to their own choices and that I guarantee them to guide them and provide them with the choices they make individually which is then as friends, as brothers and as family.

I received another video call; it lasted about two minutes. Still, I had not had a face-to-face chat on a video call. So far, all video calls had been "Hi beautiful, What are you doing? How has your day been? We will be together soon!" Then it would end with "I love you," then abruptly ended.

Erick: You look beautiful Darling.

Me: I looked like a hot mess I am doing laundry and house work.

Erick: I want you to feel free to completely show and teach me what love is in your world. you can be assured that I am a man of my word and my word is my bond.

Me: I believe you never doubted that. I try to always see the good in people and to give them the chance to prove themselves before passing judgement.

Erick: This new path is a choice that we both decided to em-

bark upon together so lets keep our eyes on the prize.
Me: Ditto
Erick: Beautiful after I asked you some personal questions, your answers are the connection that I need and the message in your eyes say you are genuinely ready for a new chapter.
Me: I am ready are you?
Erick: That's true and I believe that's the solid foundation you need, the height of a house is determined by the foundation. That's also because I know your soul is home for my heart so I feel free to express myself.
Me: That is sweet!
Erick: We are going to spend time with each other talking about us really and freely expressing how we feel with each other, for me I will love you to move in with me and my dream is to marry you and build my world with you so you can move in with me.
Me: I am considering either a transfer to another base or early retirement I need to weigh my options.
Erick: Alright my love, have you found out how much your cash out will be?
Me: I don't know that information till I decide what process I want to do. It depends on the time frame for me to make the move. All things need to be taken into consideration.
Erick: You have to decide what you want to do with your retirement personally. Do you have savings?
Me: I have a little savings
Erick: There's an investment opportunity that guarantees the future with the dividends. I can advise you to invest on it and then allow it to grow over the years while we focus on building our home.
Me: Sounds like a plan to me.
Erick: Yes, honey do you think you will be ready to move in with me by May?
Me: We can only hope to be together by then. I have no control over the process once I decide which decision to make.

If transfer is not a option then I have to apply for the early retirement and then I am on their timeline and I have no idea how long that will take.

Erick: Do you need any assistance from me, my darling? Do we need to get storage for you?

Me: I might think about liquidating most of my property and can store the items I choose to keep with my brother.

Erick: Alright my love, do you really need the clothes? Do you have pictures of your furniture?

Me: I will need some clothes! I will donate a lot but I will need some to make due till I get to where we are going to live. I do not have pictures of my furniture. But I would rather sell it as oppose to storing it. I will keep my clothes to a minimum and just personal photos and important papers. Is that sufficient?

Erick: Alright my love, I want you to take advantage of an investment opportunity in investing in lithium so while we are building a life your investment is growing.

At this point we made the decision that I would move in with him and start a life together. I did not realize at the time he was investigating me to see what I had as far property and what my net worth was. At the time, I thought he was thinking as a financial investor, not as a love interest. But now I see there would be beautiful love notes, then the money questions would start. He was very consistent with his pursuit of my financial situation. What I did not realize was that he had several other women he was scamming consecutively along with me. So when he had to go to work, supposedly at an office, he was busy working on the other victims, or clients, as he called us. I know he mentioned one as an office manager, and he had three offices within the US that he worked out of. So, when he mentioned working or a trip, he must have had others. He needed to spend more time on convincing others to give up their life savings too.

Me: I will consider investing opportunity.

Erick: I love you my queen, we will continue in the morning.

I will love you to invest about $30,000 in the investment and I will support you, then give away some of the clothes and things you don't need as seed. I was checking the best investment opportunity available for you my love. Then you will pray who you want as your beneficiary.

Me: I will consider your proposal but I have not considered the beneficiary part yet.

Erick: I will begin to process you as my beneficiary as well from tomorrow I have to make to make a few calls to my lawyer. Have you ever been arrested before?

Me: No! I have never been arrested, I have a clean record. You cannot work for the government and have a record. I have had traffic tickets but they are since gone.

Erick: Alright, my love. I believe you my love.

Me: My line of work requires you to be a honest individual. I am a law abiding citizen.

Erick: That's good and I know that you are more concerned with leaving a good legacy anywhere you go. I will have one of my team begin to process you as a private lithium investment and we take it from there my love!

Me: Ok, you take care of business and I will take care getting ready to move I have a lot of work to do until then. I need to get my retirement process started with a target date of May.

Erick: Alright my wife, we will continue tomorrow ok, I love you.

The next morning, I received two incoming video calls. My phone was on charger and turned off while I slept. I also received another photo of his dog Zeus sleeping and snoring. I still did not think anything of him pursuing me on investing because I thought he was looking ahead for our future. I was a little disturbed at him asking me if I was ever arrested but then thought he was thinking of incorporating me into his business.

Erick: Is everything ok honey>

Me: Yes, I was exhausted are you back from the gym.

Erick: Yeah honey, you have been quiet on me this morning. Are you Ok?

Me: Yes, do you have time to talk before work?

Erick: I miss you my queen, yes I have sometime for you always.

Me: I notified my boss I am retiring and I have to get the paperwork together as soon as possible to hit our deadline of middle of May. I will need your address for to complete all my paperwork and process it with the new address.

Erick: 401b Ville Drive, Boulder City, NV 89005 Las Vegas here. You need also NY address honey?

Me: Las Vegas address will be fine that will be main residence. How was your morning?

Erick: I miss you honey

Me: I miss you too! Are you at home?

Erick: Yeah honey but I'm ready to drive to work. What is your plan for the day? My Precious

Me: Taking care of some personal business then work later.

Erick: Alright my love, What time are you leaving the house?

Me: For work 7:30 P.M. EST

Erick: Alright my love

Me: I loved the Zeus video you know I have 2 cats they are part of the package will that be a problem?

Erick: My love we have enough room, Ok. Make a list of things you will love to come with, OK

Me: Just some clothes and personal items and the cats.

Erick: Alright love, I saw some videos of the last Christmas with my late wife.

Me: Are you OK? You know if you are having second thoughts about this arrangement I can back everything up. I love you and we can take things slow.

Erick: I love you too honey and I will contact you later when I get to office and am free OK?

Me: Ok, babe!

Erick: My precious, how are you doing?

Dorothy Harding

>**Me:** Busy day, just finished talking with my sister, how was your day?
>**Erick:** Alright love, have you told them about me yet my love? **Me:** My sister knows everything, I have yet to talk to my brother. Because I work nights and sleep during the day sometimes its hard to communicate with them.
>**Erick:** Alright beautiful, I have also spoken to my brother and my mom.
>**Me:** Are they happy for you?
>**Erick:** Yes, honey but mom needs more pictures of you honey.

I sent him four pictures of myself; they were headshots only. I assumed they were for his mother to see what I looked like but was unaware of any other intentions of the use of my photos. It's known that they ask for photos to possibly use to set up fake accounts and identification or for identity theft. But, to this day, my identity has not been stolen. I research my photo and do credit checks on a monthly basis since learning this. It is well known among us victims that once you're a victim, they can use other means to victimize you. I will discuss this later towards the end of this book. Up until now, I had no idea I was involved with a scammer.

>**Erick:** Thank you, honey! Zeus knows you are coming and I am going to tell the boys that I have decided that you come to live with me and us. Honey please I need your ring size again?
>**Me:** 5 ½ was the last sizing for my ring finger, babe.
>**Erick:** I just forwarded your ring size to my jeweler, honey.

(Three photos of him in a classroom setting was sent to me. One was a face selfie with others in the background, and the other pictures were him at the front of class instructing. He said he does classes on financial advising.)

>**Erick:** Honey do you like shopping?
>**Me:** Of course what female doesn't?
>**Erick:** Alright honey noted. I've spoken to one of my assistants and she has begun processing your listing as an investor

with lithium producing company Ok?
Me: When is your birthday, Erick?
Erick: June 15, 1960 when is yours honey?
Me: October 18, 1959. There is 8 months difference between us, Babe!
Erick: Hahaha, your still my baby girl.

(I sent him a video of me talking to him and blowing kisses.)

Erick: Honey, I was forwarding your video to my mom. You look beautiful, my darling! Thanks for the kisses.
Erick: I found some videos of my last memory of my late wife I would love to share with you.
Me: I would love to see them.

(3 videos were sent each with a different caption: Our last concert together, Her last birthday, Our last Christmas experience together.)

Me: Those are beautiful videos.
Erick: But this is the past now I wanted to just assure you that I am ready for a fresh start now and to enjoy loving my woman and I enjoy to be loved by her as well.
Me: I promise to love you if not as much but more than you love me, Mr. Andersen.
Erick: No woman has ever told me that, honey! And I have no doubt whatsoever that you will keep your word! I love completely honey. I will support with the moving process any way I can.
Me: How is Zeus? I am interested in seeing how she reacts to the cats.

(A photo of Zeus the French Bull dog chewing on the end of the toilet brush was sent.)

Erick: This is what I caught her doing earlier!

Me: It is going to be a daily adventure with Zeus and the 2 cats.

Erick: Hahaha, Lucky I have a big space. We can extend some space as a playground for them. Honey, my assistant told me your application has been filled, OK! So you have any idea when you can get your hand on your money to invest it?

Me: I do not know it has not been processed yet that's why I asked for your address earlier because I do not know if it will be direct deposit or in check form and I have not been given a time frame yet not till they out process me.

Erick: Alright, my precious I will speak with my staff to process which is the best platform to receive your investment fund in your case my love.

He sent me a link to a blog titled "The Best Investment Opportunities For The Future Recommended By blogspot.com," but as of now, the link no longer exists. It contained a report of several investment opportunity to invest in, one of which discussed lithium investing. I also assumed he would shut down all connections once he was discovered to be a scammer by another victim.

Erick: I want you to read through this blog from my company branch in London. It will help you to have a ground understanding also of what your money will be invested into OK.

Me: Ok, I will read it when I have a chance, Ok.

Erick: Alright honey, when was the last time you went lingerie shopping?

Me: It has been awhile, Is there good lingerie shops there?

Erick: Yes honey and I know some good lingerie tailored shops in Milan.

Me: Good!

Erick: Do you wear perfume?

Me: Yes, I do but not the cheap perfumes I like expensive ones. Black Opium by Yves Saint Laurent, Coco by Chanel, Candy

by Prada and Angel by Thierry Mugler are my favorites.
Erick: Noted, Honey!

I did not realize it at the time but later learned that when he said noted, he was actually keeping notes on what we discussed; it was probably to keep each of us victims separate so he did not mix us up. That way, he could keep track of what he said or information taken from each of us. I later knew of me and two others, but it is known they can have up to ten on the hook at the same time. I would not doubt if he had more later because what seemed like constantly communicating between us seemed to drift off later at times during our relationship.

Erick: What is your attitude toward sex in your family? Was it talked about? Who taught you about sex?
Me: My parents never discussed sex I learned about my period through a class at school. Back then they had classes regarding puberty. My parents were very modest they had to Inspect my clothes before I left the house and I was not allowed to date until I was 16 years old and I had a curfew I had to learn about sex like most other kids.
Erick: I'm a PK's son (Preacher Kids) so you know the topic is a no-no anywhere near my house hahaha. Do you use sex to self medicate? If something upsets you, do you use sex to try and Help you feel better?
Me: No, I have never had sex to self medicate or to make myself feel better. I have to have some chemistry with my partner to have sex with them.
Erick: Honey, I want you to do a little research on bitcoin my love, OK?
Me: Ok, whenever I get a chance I will look it up.
Erick: I am on the phone with my Mom telling her about us. Would you like a personal room?
Me: Personal room? You mean a separate room?
Erick: My mom was suggesting maybe you might just need to gradually settle into our room if you feel like it.

Me: That is a sweet suggestion, she might feel we are moving too fast but we will cross that path when we get together.
Erick: We will let our hearts guide us on that, my darling. If you or family have questions please ask honey any questions. I really want to meet my new family. Mom said we either come see her or she will come visit us.
Me: I will leave that up to you, Mr. Andersen
Erick: How much do you know about bitcoin?
Me: It is a digital currency is all I know that it can be used as a form of payment.
Erick: That's right smart you have a beautiful mind. I can't wait to put my crown on you. And you can also use it to receive payment. I want you to study more and let me guide you on your first transactions because your investment payments and investment is top privacy and the dividends of your investment will be paid via bitcoin, Do you understand?
Me: Ok, I will check into bitcoin when I get a chance, love.
Erick: Alright my love and I will guide you on any knowledge you need as a family too. I prefer to give you family budgets through our family bitcoin accounts.
Me: Sounds like a plan I am excited about our life together and am ready to learn about finances especially family budgets.
Erick: Thank you, my love. I also want you to know that your opinions matter a lot and feel free always to share your opinion OK?
Me: I promise to always give you my best judgement, love
Erick: I have no doubt whatsoever my darling.

In these conversations you noticed he mentioned me or my family and if we ever had any questions, just ask. But unless he was comfortable with the question, he would answer it, and if he had no answer, he would completely ignore it. It became a pet peeve with me because I am a straightforward person; if you ask me a question, whether you like the answer or not, I will answer it honestly. I uncovered a lot of info regarding how these romance scammers operate and they work on a script. This explains why he could not answering certain questions when I asked. I must have thrown him off his script. I have seen, especially on Facebook, they have Scammers Only pages that they buy and sell these scripts, so they do exist! I am not scared to investigate, and I learn daily something new. I learned a lot from talking with other victims because we realized even though our stories are different, there are similarities too. Keep in mind, these are private conversations between us that are kept private. It helps to talk to someone who experienced what you did; we don't judge one another just support. Also, privacy matters after you had your life ripped apart by one of these scammers. So, for that reason only, my story is being told, but I will divulge publicly known sources in this book and quote sources with permission. Most of us victims had judgement already passed by those we have told. We are not totally stupid and naïve, and none of us had prior knowledge of scammers. This story is to show how unsuspecting I was and how manipulative these professional thieves are. Pass judgement only after you read my story.

>**Erick:** I want to tell you how happy and please with your steps and I am also making my world ready to welcome you honey. Do you like art works?
>**Me:** Anything for the end game for us our new life together. I love art I think most creative people do!
>**Erick:** Have you ever gone to an art exhibition?
>**Me:** I have been to a lot of art exhibitions. We have a beautiful big Detroit Institute of Art Museum and to smaller Art Galleries and to Art Fairs and smaller venues. I like paintings, photos and statues.
>**Erick:** That's nice and do you have any collection or would you like to own some?
>(I have a beautiful three-foot solid cement angel statue that I sent him a picture of! I still own it to this day.)
>**Me:** My angel, I had a lot of these but my ex-husband kept most in the divorce plus they are very heavy to lift. I love hand painted crafts too.
>**Erick:** Beautiful, where did you get this one?

Me: My brother-in-law employer owned a lawn and garden place with cement statues and artwork we bought a total of 7 pieces from this angel, black bear, dog, 2 lions, eagle, elephant. The angel was the lightest item we later added more items purchased elsewhere.
Erick: Beautiful! What do you intend to do with her?
Me: I would love to bring her with us if possible. She has always brought me luck.
Erick: Do you want to bring her to our house?
Me: I would love that she is my guardian angel that's what I call her.
Erick: That is very sweet then it will give me joy to welcome her. Do you make any sacrifices to her?
Me: No, I do not make sacrifices to her. I do not believe in that type of religion. She is a protective type angel one to watch over you not to bow too.
Erick: We can have her by the pool, when you come we will decide honey.
Me: She would look beautiful by a pool, babe.
Erick: I just forwarded her picture to my mom she is asking if she can also get her, hahaha
Me: Awww, does she want her?
Erick: Yeah, my precious
Me: That can be arranged we can always purchase more angels for us.
Erick: You know where we can honey?
Me: They have a lot of the cement statues places here, babe.
Erick: Alright honey maybe we can check on some when I come before we leave there on our way back. Do you want us to fly or drive?
Me: Tell your mom we will give her my angel as a gift. What is best for you? Flying or Driving? **Erick:** Awww, you kidding me right? Do you like a road trip?
Me: I told you I love to travel we could do a road trip, last year I did a road trip driving over 1400 miles.

Erick: Hahaha, now we have to decide together in this, my love. Do you know the driving duration here to your city?
Me: Google says 1700 miles
Erick: That should be around 15 hours if I am not mistaking, honey.
Me: That would take 2 days one-way plus you would want to spend a couple days here too. even if you flew here and rented a vehicle and drove back there you are looking at 4 or 5 days.
Erick: So, you need about a week, my love?
Me: Can you spare a week?
Erick: I want you to know that you are the woman I sort of seek out and I found a beautiful, bold, smart, optimistic, committed, adventurous, philanthropic, caring and loves children. initially most women who texted me were all impatient they were so much in a rush to see. I didn't want that rush that is why I chose internet dating. To find a patient woman that is willing to take our time to know each other because I'm a very private man and that patience is one of your qualities.
Me: You are more than I could have asked for in a future partner. You seem very patient, intelligent and gifted man. I would be honored to spend the rest of our lives together. I have never thought of online dating, let alone meet such a beautiful soul as yourself and I have high expectations. How else could you explain meeting someone and falling in love with them before ever physically touching.
Erick: This is what happens when you allow your steps to be aligned with the oath of your destiny, honey.
Me: It is truly a blessing to have met one another at this time in our lives. I will never take life for granted and live up to gods expectations.
Erick: Thank you for your assurance honey and I have no doubt whatsoever. I cannot wait to solemnized with you. I will walk with unshaken confidence, with the look of a beau-

tiful sparrow and a special compartment my precious.
Me: That is beautiful, babe
Erick: My love as I walk down the aisle on that day, our first kiss will be unrushed and with distinctive taste. I promise you and unforgettable first kiss as you board certified wifey.
Me: Awww, I am looking forward to the day we finally meet. I cannot wait for that special day.
Erick: I hope your day is going well, my love.
Me: Everyday above earth is a blessing but the best part of the day is spending time talking with you.
Erick: On the day we will recite our vows, I'll look into your eyes to let you know how passionate I am about each word I'll be speaking to you. I'll accompany. My world is in excitement.
Me: You are such a romantic, my love. And I am excited and blessed.
Erick: I am too, Honey
Me: It is starting to snow here and I am completing my retirement paperwork.
Erick: My queen, Your shining. Thank you for the beautiful picture and in the midst of nervousness I won't fail to give you an assuring look and a warm and gentle gesture to let you know that everything is going to be fine. I know we are not perfect but I'm ready to hold your hands through any storm and will do everything to put a smile on your face.
Me: I just had my picture done for my passport renewal. I am so excited for our future together.

I just received eleven pictures of him outside of a winery with four other men. He also took several pictures of the winery inside and of the food and drinks they were served. This was at 10:30 P.M. at night my time.

Erick: This was earlier today, honey. What you sent was the most beautiful word to say to my soul.
Me: Those are awesome pictures is that a vineyard or distill-

ery?

Erick: Earlier today at wine cellar and tasting room. Honey, I miss you and I know soon we will be holding hands together and enjoying the love that we have been blessed with faith.

Me: I like you in blue that is a good color on you, babe

Erick: Did you eat, honey?

Me: Yes, I had a salad earlier and a chicken wrap.

Erick: What pet would you think of to own if you ever had a chance to?

Me: A horse

Erick: Have you brought time to study about bitcoin?

Me: I have not had anytime yet. I will later today if I get a chance.

Erick: I know you've been very busy, my love. I am having the cupping therapy today, honey.

Me: Really! Wow, you will have to tell me how it works afterwards, love

Erick: Yes, I will honey, though I know we are going to have our own massages together. Honey, have you ever had a helicopter city tour before?

Me: Yes, I have in the Smoky Mountains a long time ago.

Erick: Nice honey, where would you like to experience it again.

Me: Anywhere with you, my love **Erick:** As I behold your face while I walk up to you, my eyes will forever be steadfast on you. This also means that throughout our life together, my focus will be on you alone and not the problem or challenges that we may be facing.

Me: I feel the same for you, my love

Erick: No memory will be made as much as the one we will make on the day when we are finally together. You will live to cherish the days after. I love you and there is no fear in love. This I knew when I fell helplessly in love with my late wife and now I found my destiny and completeness in you. I'm ready to rock your world forever, my dearest beautiful queen. My favorite gifts from me to you everyday will be the love I promise to shower you that will draw helpless tears of love and the piercing look of a man in love. I love you my queen. I cannot wait to experience our honeymoon, as it will be more than a life in the moon but an untold bliss in the presence of the one I truly love.

Me: You have a beautiful soul, Mr. Andersen. I cannot wait to spend my new chapter of this life with you.

Erick: In the morning, when I should be seeing the sun, all I want to see is you. At night when I should behold the moonlight, your face is all I want to see. I can assure you that our home will be as bright as the morning and as cool as the night. I Erick Andersen can assure you of that!

Me: You melt my heart with your declarations, my love.

Erick: Let's look together to our future together and commit to jointly sowing the seeds of the fruits we reap because there lies our happiness. When I found you, I found a bottomless well of good wishes that can never run dry in any season. I love you my Donna!

Me: I love you my poetic soulmate

Erick: Even though there is much to fear as we choose to use internet dating and you and I know how much shady people are on there yet we are unwavering about our decision of a lifetime together. With you by my side, I am not afraid of forever. I want to assure you that I will never let you down!

Me: I have a good feeling that despite the bad in the world we can make it a better place together as long as you are by my side.

Erick: I want to take my time slow with you. I don't want to see the end of this. Eternity will be our destination. My gift to give you in your heart is made in rare stones. Stones of happiness, evergreen memories and faithfulness. I am in your life to give you another life and that is the life of love. I cannot wait to put my ring on your finger before everyone. The most solid place to stand in is in love. Love never breaks the heart, rather it mends the heart. I know my heart is safe with you forever.

Me: I cannot wait to be by your side and love you for the rest of my life in this last chapter of our lives. This has to be the very best part of our lives preparing us for eternity and as long as we continue to love and respect one another our live together will be nothing short of amazing and everyday together will be a beautiful day.

Erick: Love is a powerful weapon. I never knew you before but when my heart is ready to love it brought you from afar to me. With love, all hidden treasures can be brought to the open however, only to the one to whom it is meant for. My fiancé, you are my treasure! Our truest nature is unknown until we fall in love. I love what I see in you. It is so true and pure.

Me: I am truly honored to be chosen to be by your side, you are truly gifted. In this day and age where more and more anger and rage appear. God works in mysterious ways and I think when we truly need love in our hearts he has brought us together. If this is his wish we will become a power of one not as separate entities.

Erick: I love how you assure me that you are trusting me to lead our journey. Your words take away my fears and worries. Your character gives me assurance that our vows will be our bond forever.

Me: I hope to inspire you to be the very best you can be and I hope you will guide us always in the right direction and eliminate any fears and worries that might arise along the way during our time together here on earth. There is a saying love can move mountains lets see how many mountains we can move.

Erick: I have confidence in you, my love and I love you, my queen. My love is there anything you want me to buy and keep in the house for you?

Me: Anything I need we will buy together when I arrive as of now I only need you.

Erick: Awww, my love, I love you my precious and I'm over delighted. Honey, do you have a bible?

Me: Yes, in fact I have two one I received when I was baptized and one I received when my father died from our family pastor.

Erick: That is nice, beautiful when were you baptized?

Me: January 1975 when my father was diagnosed with bone cancer. I received the family bible when my mother died my aunt had it but I gave it to my niece so that it would be passed down through our family of generations. You know my family used bibles as keepers of treasured memories. My mother kept death notices, birth notices and wedding invitations in her bible and so did my grandparents. But I pulled those out and kept those before I gave the bible to my niece.

Erick: Oh wow, honey you are a treasure keeper. What is your favorite scripture honey?

Me: Psalm 23: The lord is my shepherd; I shall not want. He makes me lie down in green pastures. He leadeth me beside still waters. He restoreth my soul, he leads me in paths of righteousness for his names sake. Even though I walk through the valley of the shadow of death. I will fear no evil: for thou art with me; thy rod and thy staff they comfort me. Thou preparest a table before me in the presence of mine enemies: thou anoint my head with oil; my cup runneth over. Surely goodness and mercy shall follow me all the days of my life: and I will dwell in the house of the lord forever.

Erick: Can we meditate on that?

Me: Yes

Erick: It means that your creator guides you as a shepherd would guide his sheep passionately to green pastures and watch you over wild wolves on your path. Even when you walk through and act under ignorance or your weakness to your body, he watches over you. all these are words of promises to every human born by flesh, born upon this earth that is now ruled by principalities and powers in heavenly places

that are seeking to deny mankind the joy he should enjoy as a seed of our creator. This it the mindset that should dwell in us when we are to be born again.
Me: That is a beautiful metaphor, babe. Sweet dreams, my love.
Erick: I will dream of us, my love!

During the early stages of this relationship, he mentioned he was a son of a preacher. He mentioned scriptures quite often. He never acknowledged what religion he worshiped. I just assumed Christianity due to his beliefs. I do not know if this was true or if he was playing off the fact that I acknowledged being a big believer in God. I do not know how much was scripted or if he was winging it as we went along. I was always a big believer in the phrase "In every lie, lies the truth." But, then again, I now know he was a professional scammer. I will state this many times that I am a curious soul by nature, and I would have liked to know who the real person was behind this persona he perpetuated. That would have brought me closer. In the end, that is all we victims seek besides "Why me?"

Erick: Good Morning, Beautiful> How are you doing this morning?
Me: I am at the hospital visiting my Aunt, she had surgery. I also am informing some family that I am moving and getting married in the near future.
Erick: That's a confirmation my love because I also just finished speaking with my brother and he said he will be at hand to welcome you. What did they say my love?
Me: They seem happy for me, my love. I only seen my Uncle briefly he was heading out as I was arriving.
Erick: Ok love, you didn't tell him?
Me: No, we only spoke briefly, babe.
Erick: I am excited to meet him, Did you tell him about us?
Me: No, we just spoke and he walked away you would have to chase him down to hold a extended conversation with him. What time is your cupping appointment?

Dorothy Harding

> **Erick:** Hahaha honey! I am already preparing myself honey.

(He sent me a picture of him with a T-shirt and knit shorts on and barefooted.)

> **Me:** Oh, your there you have cute legs!
> **Erick:** Hahaha, you flatter me darling! I am blessed to have the most beautiful woman with an amazing soul.
> **Me:** Your lucky to have a woman with good taste in men.
> **Erick:** Honey do you like to celebrate anniversaries?
> **Me:** Of course, do you?
> **Erick:** Alright my love, yes I do my love. Have you ever had sex in the mall before?
> **Me:** No, I usually never shopped with my ex-husband in the mall.
> **Erick:** I have had sex in the mall with my late wife, it was on our engagement anniversary. we decided to go shop presents for us collectively then while we were in fitting area I decided to go in and watch her change and I could not control myself and had to seduce her and she bent over and the rest you know what they say what happens in Rome stays in Rome.
> **Me:** Sorry babe, I just got home and read your message. How was the cupping?

He sent two pictures of him lying face down with the cups on his back. It became uncomfortable at times, because he would bring up stories of he and his late wife. I have yet to meet a woman who would have been comfortable with these conversations. I just would not respond instead of saying something. He never said much about how she died, only that it was roughly five years ago. No information on how she died either. I just listened hoping to pick up some clues. I had asked him several times if he was actually over her and ready to move forward, as you will see during some of our conversations. Later, he rarely brought her up. I guess it wasn't in the script.

> **Me:** Wow, did it work? I heard they heat them up before they put them on, did it hurt?
> **Erick:** They will be pulled shortly then I will show you, Ok

my love?
Me: Ok, babe

(Three more pictures came through of him shirtless with the red circles where the cups were.)

Me: How did it feel? Did it hurt? Nice body babe
Erick: Yeah, it was painful but feels good
Me: How long did it take? How long does the welts last?
Erick: The good thing is that it was revealed (by the color of the stain) that I have good circulation. I feel new and I keep burning fat and increasing muscle mass. It was for and hour but I wanted to rest my head as well so I enjoyed the process.
Me: Awesome, my love. I am glad it went well for you and that you have good circulation. I am busy with getting everything organized and I was looking at so wedding gown styles too.
Erick: That's sweet honey, that means we also have to increase our plans. I have a wedding planner that organized the wedding of my colleague that introduced me to Zoosk. that is where he met his wife and the wedding was fantastic.

Three more pictures were sent of the wedding of his supposed colleagues, but I now know they were more stolen photos from the family he had been using to seduce me and others. I feel awful every time I look at these photos because they represent dollar signs for scammers and fraud for me and the victims. This is something that most people don't understand! We were defrauded or catfished into to giving up our hard-earned money.

Me: Babe, I don't want a large wedding but a small personal wedding. What are your thoughts? All that matters is to be your wife in front god.

(Three more wedding pictures was sent with captions.)

65

Erick: My late wife's step sister's wedding.

Me: I love her dress it is beautiful

Erick: would you like us to involve a wedding planner my love?

Me: I think the venue and reception would be fine but the wedding party we should be able to organize ourselves. I would like a simple outdoor venue. What are your thoughts?

Erick: It will give us room to do us and I will even want to invite a special band from my country. you can make a list of things you have in mind and share with me as a list so that I can have it in on my side ok!

Me: Of course, I will that way we can plan our wedding together. I would love to have a band from your country incorporated into our wedding. I want it to reflect our love and personalities after all this is our day right?

Erick: That's right my precious and I am already excited and I feel happy now that you feel this Way, honey. I believe that god put us as men here on earth to care after his most sacred Creature women. Can you dance kizomba?

Kizomba is a dance from Angola. It is absolutely an African dance. The music we dance to, also called Kizomba, comes from a long tradition of samba music that encountered influences from Caribbean zouk and new electronic sounds in the late 70's and early 80's. This description is from Social Dance community website. socialdancecommunity.com. Because Bahamas has influence from African roots I never thought about maybe he might be a Nigerian. That being said I was raised in Detroit which is Motown sound. Detroit has R&B, Soul, and Blues mixed influences. So to each his own on musical influences.

Me: No, but you can teach me, Mr. Andersen.

Erick: You know it will give me joy, my darling. I teach my boys that every woman is an angel and should be treated as an angel keeper so that you can receive the gifts of her angelic

heart. I want you to love you the way you deserve to enjoy love, my queen. Do you have any honeymoon wishes?
Me: Tropical, babe
Erick: I want you to choose that, OK?
Me: South Pacific Islands would be wonderful. I want you all to myself no tourists.
Erick: That's my desire, my love
Me: What are you doing, Babe?
Erick: I'm resting and discussing with your mother-in-law. What did you learn on the bitcoin?
Me: How it is processed, transferred between parties as a form of currency.
Erick: Honey, I want you to listen to my advice as I rally around you and see how much you can raise at least this week to begin your first bitcoin experience and to book your investment spot of the opportunity while we are still arranging you coming to the house and for our wedding also. You know many more beautiful hotel resorts and shops are already accepting bitcoin as a means of payment. Do you understand what I mean honey?
Me: Yes, I do and I will follow your advice and I will count on you to walk me through my first experience with bitcoin. How much do you think I would need to get started?
Erick: My queen, I don't know what you are capable of investing right now this week to begin. what do you think you can begin with my love?

From the beginning, he posed as a financial investment specialist. He had a detailed website and a LinkedIn page. I had no doubt at this time that he was not whom he portrayed to be. When he brought up investing to me, he was selling it as for our future together. He also said the money that was to be invested was mine, not for his personal income. I was looking for additional income for retirement. So all money discussed was him showing me what the best investment opportunities were available for our future together.

Me: Is $500 ok to start?

Erick: That's ok my love but I will advise you to take a better step, OK? You will see the reason why as you progress with your steps believe me. You think I don't know that you are more gifted than you think you are? Sleep over how much more intelligently and boldly you want to invest to begin this new path of knowledge and smartness so that this week you can begin. Then you can decide how you want your bridal train so we can begin preparing for our future. My brother said he will be my best man!

Me: I will my love, I am happy your brother will be your best man.

Erick: This is the point my family have been praying for me. I'm not kidding you my love. You coming to our home you will see the love that awaits you. If this is my last opportunity to be married again and I want to give it my best shot and enjoy everyday like it is my last.

Me: I have no doubts about your intention. I love you and I want us to guide one another with peace and understanding especially during our transitional time in our lives. I am falling more in love with you everyday and I hope our future is filled with love, kindness and patience.

Erick: I promise you my endless love if that's what you will ever remember me for my darling As long as I live. I have so much assurance in your soul and I can only pray for the favor Of God upon you more and more, my love.

Me: I love you, my soulmate.

Erick: Have you read your bible yet today? I want you to take the time to read a scripture my love, OK?

Me: You have one in particular you want me to visit?

Erick: My love, I want you to read Colossian 3:15, Ok

Me: Ok, my love I will meditate also.

Erick: I have heard so much about meditation and that begins with reading a scripture for the day and saying the versus from the bible that aligns my faith and convictions in the love of god for me and my family and tell me how grateful I am for all he has and his doing for me. Then tell him I'm available to be used as a vessel to bring the fulfillment of his kingdom wishes her on earth and then ask him to faithfully provide my daily bread and forgive my sins that I will commit consciously or unconsciously and then ask him to give me grace to forgive those that will error against me again. I need to seek his protection every step I take and then he will teach me how to love those around me and to complete his purpose for my life.

Me: When I go through a rough time and I know our god and his angels are there for me. It is like having spiritual insurance. All you have to do is believe in him and live your life right under his eyes. After my divorce I attended church religiously but I felt more closer to him one on one. I do not need to attend services to be close to god and heaven.

Erick: You see that you and I are coming together to form a great generation.

Me: I am looking forward to a future filled with love and happiness with you.

Erick: It's only a duty I will be honored to carry on with pride all the days of my life, my love. This I promise you.

Me: I am excited for our journey to begin. What are you doing, Erick?

Erick: I am going through my wardrobe to bring out clothes that I don't need any more from my closet to give to my gardener. You will meet him also I have told him about you already.

Me: You have such a beautiful heart to think of others in that way. I have a younger girl at work who does not have extra and I give her some clothes I no longer wear that are in excellent shape. She has a young baby to care for and if you are working hard for your family you deserve to have something nice to wear.

Erick: You see that you and I come from the same world, my love. I know

Me: Most definitely from the same world, with the same grateful souls

Erick: That's right my precious and I know I was going to find you and my faith led me to you. **Me:** And me to you, god has a reason for everything

Erick: When I say you are a soulful woman, I'm not saying to make you see your potential, when we first began to know each other and understand each other I also noticed you are very optimistic and these potentials are a very solid foundation from a woman you want to spend the rest of your life with.

Me: I am a very optimistic person, and I always believe in the good in people and there is always a new beginning when things go bad. I have never had an oppressive personality I am not a loud obnoxious person. I am a soft spoken except with laughter

Erick: Yes and your laughter was what caught the eyes of my soul. Honey, your made any progress with the gown? And the topics we left for today?

Me: I have an appointment for Tuesday at a wedding gown boutique to try on gowns. I have a lot of work to do before then.

Erick: Alright my precious, I just wanted to let you know that since I met you baby that my whole life has changed and everyone tells me that I am not the same. I want you to know that you walked into my life at the right time, however there is no good time for leaving because forever is my dream of love with you. I love you darling. You took the first step to spend forever with me, its so courageous of you hence your my queen.

Me: I feel the same about you and that gives me the courage to take the steps to be with you forever, Mr. Andersen.

I have no idea why he asked me to go try on wedding gowns to get an idea of size and style. That and the part where he actually wanted me to move in with him was to get me to liquidate my property into cash form to "invest" with him is all I can think of. I am a logical person, and at some point, I believed him instead of listening to logic, but keep in mind, I had no knowledge of Romance Scammers or how they work. He, at this point, had a logical reason for all my questions.

> **Erick:** Alright love, have you thought how much you can start up to book your investment spot my love.
> **Me:** Can it wait a couple weeks to see how much I can raise? I really want to concentrate on wrapping things up here first, babe.
> **Erick:** Alright my love your right. My concern is for you to meet the deadline. Honey, do you need me to bring some boxes?
> **Me:** No, I have plenty of boxes and totes just bring those strong arms to lift them.
> **Erick:** I'm coming with Zeus, is that OK?
> **Me:** You can bring Zeus, babe
> **Erick:** That's a must she loves to travel, but mostly road trip hahaha
> **Me:** Good that way she can get used to the cats, my love
> **Erick:** That's true babe, do you have a house for the cats?
> **Me:** I have carriers for them you cannot house them together for travel they need their own individual space.
> **Erick:** My love, you are the woman I set out to find and my joy is filled because I found you. I look forward to our progress daily, honey. Remember that we are now in the next chapter of our lives.
> **Me:** I look forward to the future.
> **Erick:** I know the blessings and favors of our creator is upon you and I know that with you By my side I am blessed. I was at the gym but I'm home and will be out for work shortly. Honey, where is the best place you can receive a present?
> **Me:** Here is my current address, babe
> **Erick:** Imagine driving to the office to meet me for a quickie

Me: That can be arranged

Erick: You are precious! Honey, how is preparation? I hope your excited my love sometimes my heart skips for joy

Me: I stay so busy that I have to remind myself to eat! I have an appointment for a fitting at a wedding boutique in the morning and I have a lot of closets to go through also on top of working full time.

Erick: Thank you my love and I'm overly excited about tomorrow wow!

Me: When your phone starts to ping you will know why! I am so excited to start a new chapter with you. I am on cloud nine despite being exhausted.

Erick: How are the cats babe? Are they also going to be ready for our lives together?

Me: Yes, they will be. They seem to sleep till I come home then go crazy. They do not understand me digging through all the closets though. I tell them every day are you ready for a daddy?

Erick: I love how you said it! I was also telling Zeus in the morning that new mommy is coming home hence the excitement also. Honey, thank you for the songs you have sent me on my way home and it gave me a peaceful drive home knowing that you will be seated by my side while we drive and enjoy the songs that we love together.

Throughout this relationship, we have sent one another our favorite songs via YouTube videos. I sent him my favorite rock, R&B, and pop songs, and he has sent me his. Originally, he stated he listened to reggae, gospel, and R&B, but he seemed to send a lot of soft pop or R&B. All seemed to be from my generation, which he claimed to be from also. When speaking on the phone, I could not distinguish his age from his voice; he seemed to have a low, soft spoken deep voice with an accent. It could very well be African dialect, but it could be Malaysian also. He seemed to like 60s R&B music, but that could be to realign with my generation also. Either way, he seemed to be intelligent and diligent about keeping up the disguise he had created. I wonder how many women he had scammed prior to me to learn the trade of deception!

Me: I cannot wait to be by your side on a long drive, babe
Erick: If you love this you should be rest assured that I also want it and we both as adults and I am telling you from the bottom of my heart that this is also what I want. I need a woman who understands me from the core of my soul, a woman I can share everything with and I look at her confidently knowing that she feels the same way about me also and I can close my eyes knowing that if I don't see the break of the following day that I know in my spirit that she will continue to rule our worlds with the same revelation into our legacy.
Me: I do understand my love but it would be sad if you were to not continue in this world without you. I consider you my soulmate and it would be horrible to think of you leaving this world too soon.
Erick: Love is the powerful tool to unite the world and it defeats the power of every hold and brings people from every part of the world together to speak one language which is happiness. Honey do you know what is bride price?
Me: No, I have never heard of it, what does it mean?
Erick: It's a celebration with the relatives of you wife, bringing them together and officially thanking them for welcoming him as a part of their family.
Me: Awww, that is beautiful!
Erick: Yes honey, Does your family observe that?
Me: No, I have never heard of this ritual until you just mentioned it. Usually there is just a Wedding Reception of both families for a mutual celebration of love and happiness for the newly married couple.
Erick: I absolutely agree and you know many have lost their peace and happiness trying to please family members. Its goo you have found your peace.
Me: Yes, I have learned you cannot please everyone in this

lifetime and its best to be honest with yourself with any family relationship that you may not be able to make everyone happy and if so, is it worth sacrificing your own happiness for! I have a huge family and we are all different and I have learned its best to keep myself happy then appease others because happiness can be contagious.

Erick: I'm sorry for that experience my love. It's not easy with any family and thanks for sharing with me. I want you to know that I have you now and I will not allow you to feel any pain. your confidence sends me into a bliss of love. Your words send me into your arms and set fire on my heart. I love you my chosen fiancé.

Me: I love you my beloved soulmate and soon to be husband.

Erick: Sit here and look into the future. All I see is a pure confident beautiful and loving woman with a visionary man living the life of their dream and sharing the same mission. We are that happy couple in my dream, babe!

Me: I have no doubt we will be a happy couple together and all our dreams will come true, Mr. Andersen

Erick: I want to always bring upon you a strength that you never knew you had. I want to always accentuate the beauty in you that has been downplayed. Your love was the best thing that ever happened to me, it made me the man I becoming daily, my love.

Me: I love you, my beautiful soulmate

Erick: Let's look together to the future, cause there lies our happiness. When I found you I found a bottomless well of good wishes that can never run dry in any season. I love you, my love.

Me: I love you too, babe. Let's plan our life filled with happiness and love that we both deserve. You will become my everything in this new chapter we are creating in this life and I hope to make you the happiest man alive.

Another incoming phone call that did not connect. I assumed they were phone calls, but they were VOIP calls, Voice Over Internet Protocol, which is a technology that allows you to make voice and video calls using broadband internet connection instead of a regular phone line. They allow you to call anyone who has a telephone number, including local, long distance, mobile, and international numbers. Also, some VOIP services only work over your computer or special VOIP phone; other services allow you to use a traditional phone connected to a VOIP adapter. This is according to www.fcc.gov. The problem is, these scammers buy and sell USA phone numbers to make these further untraceable by any means. It is impossible to trace a VOIP number with a VOIP number, especially if it says the number used is from another country other than which the call is actually made. This allows them to further their criminal activity. Erick used five numbers during our relationship. I have spoken with him personally on four of the numbers; the fifth one I discovered later. That way, he can manipulate several victims at once and keep track of us all.

Me: Babe, here are your pictures of me trying on wedding gowns.

(I sent thirteen shots of different styles of wedding gowns to him as requested from him.)

Erick: Wow, I'm ready to change my life for you in order to be the best husband for you. I am ready to take on new responsibilities and challenges and I am ready to do you proud all because all my life I have been made ready for you my precious wife, my love. you are beautiful, do they have a crown also.
Me: I did not try on any veils or crowns they had a lot of vintage accessories.
Erick: Honey have you left there already?
Me: Yes, I am home, babe.
Erick: You look super adorable and I'm feeling proud and I am looking forward to show you off to my world. You make me wish I was there with you. Honey, how far is the place

from your house?

Me: It took me 30 minutes with light traffic.

Erick: Do you want me to go shop with you there? There are some shops in Milan and Dubai I would love us to visit

Me: The dress attendant said it is customary to check other places and try on all dresses I like before making a final decision. She has my name and measurements etc. in case I choose one of the dresses I tried on. I would love to go to Milan and Dubai.

Erick: That is very smart of you honey and yes I would love to take you by the hand and watch you try them on also. Babe, any progress regarding your passport?

Me: I mailed my renewal in on Friday and I had it express processed so I should receive it in a couple of weeks.

Erick: Alright my love, Are you home now? Please give me your last name again I want to re-save it honey I cannot find where I saved it.

Me: Harding, my love

Erick: My love, I cannot stop looking at the pictures you sent. My mom says that you have fire of passion in your eyes.

Me: Did you show her the pictures?

Erick: Yes, of course my love and she said she is going to begin shopping for her own outfit for the wedding as well, hahaha

Me: Awww, that is so sweet, I cannot wait to meet her, babe

Erick: She's already excited to meet you, my love What are you doing?

Me: Watching the news, I hate hearing the bad news of crime and hate, babe

Erick: It's inevitable my love these days and times. That's why we have to hold solidly our creator and giver of life.

Me: The violence is senseless I cannot understand how you can hurt someone you have never met or harm a innocent child but almost everyday there is violence in the news instead of good deeds.

Scammed in America

Erick: Did you hear about the shooting in a mosque in New Zealand?

Me: Yes, I think it is terrible to target anyone based on race or religion. Racism and hate is inhumane. There should be no place for that in this world. My parents have taught me humanity and to always treat one another equal. How can one person think they are better than another is disillusioned person.

Erick: That is why it is good to train a child in a way they should grow because when they are older, they will not depart from it. Then I also think to be unforgiven can also lead a lot of people to allow their emotions to cloud their sense of judgement.

Me: Hate and inhumanity is taught so is love and intolerance of hate. Unfortunately you have to train your children from a young age to defend themselves and what dangers to look out for in others to keep them from becoming victims.

Erick: We are going to live daily in expressing and sharing love in our world.

Me: The only way to beat the hate is with education and hoping love prevails. Sharing love overcomes any hate and can help a person overcome the pain. Even if it is listening to someone and showing compassion.

Erick: Yes, that is right, it is love that has endured creation.

Me: Erick, what is your favorite fruit?

Erick: Honey, I love Watermelon, do you like it?

Me: Are you kidding, I was raised on watermelon! Every family picnic we had several watermelons. I can eat a half of a seedless personal watermelon in one sitting, but it has to be ice cold but I love all fruit though.

Erick: Wow, I love all fruits also my love but watermelon has a way it cools my soul.

Me: I grew up with a apple and pear tree in the yard also a concord grape vine so during the summer months I did not even have to go inside to get a snack but of course my mother was not happy about me eating fruit off the ground or off the tree. She thought all fruit had worms in them and should be properly cleaned but she was also aware I had a terrible sweet tooth because her father, my papa was the same way. But we always had Cantaloupe, Watermelon and Honeydew melons during the hottest season.

Erick: I want to enjoy what it feels like to be loved in your world. If it is the last experience for me please make it an amazing one because I will make yours amazing that I can assure you. Why do you keep giving me limitless reasons to love you and leaving me with no choice? I love you so much and thank you for loving me, Donna.

Me: Because love can be endless between to people who understand and nourish it as partners in life. There is nothing we cannot accomplish together as one with love in our life. I cannot wait to spend the rest of my life with you, Erick!

Erick: Can you see just what you have done to me? Your love has set me on my feet, pulls my cheek so I could smile always. I love you for who you are to me now and always. I love you Mrs. Donna Andersen.

Me: Awww, My beautiful happy soul

Erick: My love I'm home from work.

(A video was sent of Zeus running to him greeting him as he came in the door.)

Me: Awww, that is sweet Zeus greets you, love.
Erick: Yeah my love, I miss you my love.

(A picture was sent of two men I assumed were his friends.)

Me: Are you having a party?
Erick: No love they called almost same time asking if you have finally come here, they want to meet you.
Me: Did you tell them you have to have me all to yourself

first that they will have to wait till May.

Erick: I told them we are busy with our arrangements, my love. I hope you are ready.

Me: Definitely, My love

Erick: I have total trust in you my love. I still cannot stop looking at your beautiful photos of you In the wedding gowns. You know which one you liked more? They all look sexy on you.

Me: I liked the champagne lace one the best, the girl that attended me said you can shorten It afterward and wear it on your 1st Anniversary.

Erick: Alright my love, Did you have sex in your wedding dreams?

Me: I dream of the wedding night, if that is what your referring to.

Erick: What is your favorite color of undies?

Me: Pink is favorite

Erick: I have that in mind now my love and I will hold your hands and enjoy every minute with you as we go through this phase of this opportunity to enjoy our wedding and to make sure we take advantage of everything that the creator wants us to go through this seeding and laying the foundations process for our lives together in love and in happiness guiding each other and fulfilling each other's heart desires with our soulmate.

(Another video was sent of his deceased wife dancing with who looks to be her father, no sound!)

Erick: Our last Christmas experience with her. I enjoy to see my world happy and happiness is always present in my home. I live by these four values Live, Laugh, Love and Life.

Me: Nice video, I can see you were very happy together. I bet you and the boys miss her still.

Erick: Yes, and you and her are the best of different worlds where you were put by destiny and I call myself favored to be chosen by destiny as the man that will enjoy the love you both very much and I will treat you as you deserve but not like her because you are both two different souls, beautiful and blessing to me. Did you have a picture of the dress you most favor the most? Honey did you feel bad with the video I sent you?

Me: No, I just need to make sure you are ready for us.

Erick: Yes, I am very ready and I want you to see that I am a happy man and enjoys having fun and I make sure my family is also filled with happiness so you can be assured of your happiness with me. I am sorry you feel down by the video my love.

Me: It has casted doubts if you are actually ready for a new chapter. She was your wife of 22 years and the mother of your children. You might not be completely ready to move forward. I am uprooting my life completely and you have to understand I have to make completely sure you are ready for us. I love you and want to spend the rest of my life with you but I have to make sure you are ready to move forward and put the past behind you. You understand what I am saying?

Erick: I understand what you mean and I realized that I might have sent you the wrong impression after I sent it to you ok and I apologize my love for any wrong impression it might have given you.

He attempted to call me; it rang but did not connect. I also started to feel that maybe I should have second thoughts about this relationship. I now realize it should have been a red flag.

Me: I don't want you to feel like you cannot talk about her with me. I am an open and honest person and you should never have to apologize for be open about your past with your late wife. I love you, babe.

Erick: I love you too. Let's meditate honey I want to read a scripture James 5:1 to the end

I thought it was odd he never comprehended meditation and looking within but considered it as Bible study. This was his version of meditation. And he never stated what religion, other than Christianity, that he belonged to.

> **Erick:** I assure you that although I am not perfect but will do my best to make you happy everyday. thank you for giving your heart to me.
> **Me:** I thank God every day for bringing you into my life, I have never been so excited to start a new chapter with a beautiful soul like yours, Mr. Andersen.
> **Erick:** Your love and your hands is all I need. I need a woman that will make an impact and make our creator proud for giving us life and I know you are that woman. I am not seeking a woman to give me money and I am not a gold digger and everything I need our creator has given to me all I need now is a woman that will complete me.
> **Me:** I can promise you a lifetime of love and happiness and to stand by your side. I was just seeking a companion to love me as much as I can love him and I received so much more. I have met a beautiful heart with a soul to match. I feel truly blessed to have met you let alone fall in love with you.
> **Erick:** Our creator knows that I need a woman like you that will accept me for who I am and love me completely and you are that woman. I love you my queen. Is there any progress today my love. Guess what happened today?
> **Me:** What happened my love?
> **Erick:** I had an online presentation and among one of the top managers was a man I met once before when I visited Alabama at a hotel. The man had been arrested by the manager of the hotel because he failed to pay his outstanding bill. I was touched and paid his bill off for him and we had never exchanged contact information and today he was able to recognize me and spoke with confidence of how he can assure that I know what I am doing.

Me: That is a beautiful story and it is good that you are an inspiration to others and this man has let you know that you did the right thing paying his tab. You inspired this man to be a better person and showed him there are truly caring people who walk among us. This gives me even more reason to fall deeper in love with you.

Erick: Honey, we are a vessel to put a smile on those who need it. Love, kindness and peace are seed that comes back to you seven fold. I know that our destiny has been written together my queen.

Me: I love you my happy soul.

Erick: Thank you for loving me. I consider myself favored, honey

A picture came through; it was a face selfie of him smiling. It is known that most of the seasoned scammers have access to Photoshop and can digitally alter pictures to suit their needs. They buy and sell information regarding any new technology that they can use to complete their con on their victims. I have seen videos of this man but not a direct face-to-face video. They take stolen videos off of Instagram or Facebook and do voiceovers if they are really good, like this one; you don't even notice. Most all the videos he had sent, words were overdubbed or silent. I have seen Facebook pages where they buy and sell programs to one another. This is a reality.

Me: You have a very handsome and sweet face, my love

Erick: My love in my dream I saw myself in a pure white background and then suddenly like a wave and I found myself in a deep well drowning and then I saw my late wife in a pure background and she came to me and then she was pulling me then I was out of the deep well and then you appeared and she took you by the hand and brought you to me and then you held me and began to clean me up and I woke up my love. beautiful wife I love you so much and I am excited to meet you and hold you. Will you ever consider plastic surgery?

Scammed in America

Me: Depends on what the plastic surgery is for

Erick: My love maybe for you to adjust any part of your body or to renew.

Me: Of course, I would consider it. What woman would not want to change any part of there body they do not like.

Erick: Alright my love but which one would you consider? Are you home, honey?

Me: Yes, I am home probably some cool sculpting maybe a facial lift, I really have not thought about it.

Erick: Honey, have you received any package today?

Me: No, but 1-800-Flowers called today

Erick: What did they say?

Me: They called asking for someone else and I did not recognize the name. I told them they had the wrong number, he seemed very confused and I hung up. He called back a few minutes later asking what my apartment number was to this address.

Erick: I sent you some flowers. Did you give me a wrong address?

Me: No, he had the right address but no apartment number you must have neglected to give them the apartment number when you ordered the flowers.

Erick: I don't think so. Can you contact them again? Because they were suppose to deliver it today.

Me: I gave him the correct address.

Erick: Alright honey, I hope they get it to you , babe!

Within two minutes of the conversation, I received a knock on the door and an azalea plant was delivered. He seemed skittish because he gave a different name on the order but had my name right. I now often wonder if that name he gave was actually the name of the scammer. I cannot remember it, only that it was not a common name. I took a picture and sent it to Erick. I was kind of thrown off because it was a plant, and we never discussed flower likes or dislikes before.

> **Me:** The plant is beautiful, babe!
> **Erick:** I am glad you like my love. I just wanted something simple to remind you everyday that I am in your life to stay. Are you off to work yet?
> **Me:** No, I leave in 40 minutes.
> **Erick:** What did you eat baby girl?

It is well known amongst us victims that all scammers ask certain questions regularly and "Have you eaten?" or "What did you eat?" are common. We believe, because most of these scammers are from third world countries, they can tell by what you eat how wealthy you are. Of course, this is unknown only to the scammers, but that is what us victims have figured out by talking amongst ourselves. That is the only reason for asking that question repeatedly. They pose as a person with knowledge, but like what I always believed, "Through every lie is an ounce of truth." My scammer has slipped and said he had just fish or just potatoes for dinner.

> **Me:** I had just a quick tuna salad before I leave for work but will cook tomorrow. I have a new recipe for crab cakes I want to try.
> **Erick:** Alright my love, I want to see a photo when you are done, Ok?
> **Me:** I will send you a picture when I make them, babe.
> **Erick:** My wife, I want you to see that in my life and my world you are the doctor. I know that of I don't see a new day that you will always love this man
> **Erick: Me:** That is a sweet metaphor, babe
> **Erick:** I keep asking myself why heaven has blessed me with you as the most wonderful gift I have ever gotten. Can I pull your cheeks? Smiles. I love you.
> **Me:** I love you and you can squeeze my cheeks anytime, babe.
> **Erick:** Thank you my love, and I am blessed and feel loved by destiny that you are the woman chosen for me. A woman that really loves me from her heart and I can feel it. I miss

you and all I know is that I'm in love with you and I can tolerate your weaknesses.

Me: My weaknesses really? What do you consider my weaknesses?

Erick: Well I don't know for now but as we will grow we will find out each other weaknesses then learn to love one another's weaknesses. Do you believe that children have rights? Do you feel that a child has a opinion that should be considered when making family decisions, such as moving or changing schools or family vacations?

Me: Of course I do! Children should be allowed to give their opinion especially if it affects them. It teaches them decision making which is needed to grow. You want your children to grow up to be happy and healthy and well-adjusted adults.

Erick: That's absolutely true and I love your response, honey. Should boys be treated the in the same way as girls? Should they have the same rules of conduct? Should you have the same expectations for their sexual behavior?

Me: Yes, boys should be treated equally as girls. There should be the same rules of conduct for both, not separate! I have a brother that is 15 months younger than me. He was allowed to stay out after dark and I wasn't! I was told because he was a boy and girls should not be out after dark. It was supposed to be for safety reasons of what society sees as the weaker gender. I believe that both boys and girls have different sexual behavior and it depends on the actual child. But educate them on the dangers that is lurking in society and the repercussions if the rules are not adhered to!

Erick: That is well said and well thought of honey because they are all human bodies with different sexual bodies. I just want to understand your opinion on some basic parenting of children. In a blended family should birth parents be in charge of making decisions for their own children?

Me: Yes, I do believe all decisions regarding your children should be yours. If you ask me my opinion or the children asks me my opinion I will give it but otherwise those are your children and your decisions should come solely from you their father. I should respect you enough to abide by your wishes for your children.

Erick: Have differences concerning conception or child raising ever been a factor for you in the breakup of a relationship?

Me: No, but I have never conceived a child. I was married to a man with 3 children from his first wife. So as a stepmother I would never interfere with his relationship with his children, but if he asked me my opinion, I would give it.

Erick: That's awesome honey and that makes you an awesome soul. How important is it that you and your partner be on good terms with each others families?

Me: It makes a happier marriage to be on good terms with one another's family. It makes for an unhappy marriage to disrespect one another families. It not only causes strain on the marriage and some have led to divorce over in-law family issues. And never compare each other families to another. You create unnecessary problems that you may not be able to overcome.

Erick: You are a well-balanced woman mentally and we are going to get along with so much understanding in this path that we have chosen to bravely embark upon with faith in our creator that he is guiding our every step into good things that we deserve as his children that believe he loves us.

Me: I have no doubt that our creator will guide us through our remaining lives. I am glad you have faith in me and in us and see a productive future together. I always believed what comes around goes around, that you reap the rewards of your hard work and maybe not immediately but eventually. If you do bad it will come back at you 10 times worse. Karma takes over. God has a special place for those who endure at the hands of others and that is why he instills patience in all mankind.

Erick: My wife every word you say touches me and guarantees me your love. Every food Our world needs today: spiritually, physically, mentally, socially, financially and Environmentally I am attracting today in Jesus name Amen!
Me: I love you, honey. What's your plans for today?
Erick: My beautiful wife I am doing some personal cleaning then I will be finalizing on my research for my presentation because I will be flying to Miami on Monday, honey!
Me: Sounds like fun
Erick: But I will find out if I am flying alone or with some of my team members, honey
Me: How long will you be in Miami, Erick?
Erick: I think 16 days it all depends on the outcome of my presentation, my love
Me: Wow, sounds nice! I hope all goes well
Erick: Thanks, my love if it all goes well it is for us. I will make you videos of my trip because I might be flying private with the team.
Me: I am looking forward to the videos, as long as your smiling face is involved
Erick: Then I will do my best to take you along every step of the way. I will even call you to say hello and you can give me a kiss before we depart. I will video if that's alright with you, my love **Me:** I always enjoy any face time with you, my love
Erick: Alright my love. I also enjoy FaceTime with you too, my queen.
Me: Are the boys going with you to Miami? Most kids are going on spring break from school
Erick: They go to Granny's from NY, honey. Because I have to work but I should see them before they go back to school.
Me: That's good they get to spend time with your mom, that is how I spent 2 weeks of my summer every year was with my grandparents.
Erick: That's an awesome feeling, my love

>**Me:** Have I told you just how blesses I am to have in my life, babe?
>**Erick:** Yes, you just did my love and I love you my queen, my co-pilot, my captain, my rib Mrs. Donna Andersen!
>**Me:** I love you, Mr. Erick Andersen
>**Erick:** I have no doubt, my love. I know my queen and I will not fail to do the same. Honey, I need you to take care of your investment spot through bitcoin before my trip, OK? So that I can handle it for you.

If you notice throughout our conversations, there was a lot of lovey dovey conversation and then "the investment" conversation arises. Not once during this year-long relationship did he just come out and ask me for money. It always followed a long love letter or "How are you doing?" "Are you taking care of yourself?" and "I am always here for you"; then "I need you to invest some money for OUR future!" Later you will see how it changed to others' needs. Also, you will see another pattern that he uses, that something bad is happening either with his mom or the boys, but there seemed to be an emergency that arose and he needed my help. This is very common in all romance scams!

>**Me:** What do you need from me?
>**Erick:** I need you to book your spot with the company and they accept your booking through bitcoin and also pay you your dividends through bitcoin so I need to guide you on how to use bitcoin to pay your spot so that we can reinvest all that you want to. You said you had $500 the last time we talked and I will advise you to increase your at the spot fund
>**Me:** I think I can increase it to $800 at the most I can invest right now. Would that be enough?
>**Erick:** I think bitcoin charges and being a first time investor you should budget about $1000, OK
>**Me:** I will see what I can do, no promises babe
>**Erick:** I have to guide you tonight or this weekend, my love. I will tell you the application to Download to start the process, OK?

Scammed in America

Me: Ok, babe I trust you to guide me through this process
Erick: Yes, I will my love. What time do you think we can try to work on this babe?
Me: I will let you know later today. I have to see where I can pull the extra $200 from
Erick: Alright my love
Me: Can the funds come from 3 different sources if so, I can do it?
Erick: What do you mean, honey?
Me: Can I use credit and debit cards to do transaction or must it come from just one form of payment?
Erick: My love on the bitcoin platform you have access to pay with credit cards Ok?
Me: So, I can use 3 separate cards for 1 transaction correct?
Erick: I think you should rather transfer the full $1000 to just one of the card accounts then use that account to make the transaction, my love
Me: Ok, then I can do $1000 for my first investment.
Erick: You understand me when I speak and that means a lot, it makes me more confident to tell you more about our destination in this relationship and knowing that you will understand me and act with every step required. I believe in you so much my love.
Me: Of course, I understand what you say, you are my soulmate and I will repeat what you say for clarification to verify, babe.
Erick: I love you my queen Donna
Me: I love to hear you talk you have a wonderful point of view and voice, Erick
Erick: My love that is sweet of you to say. I once had a ticket to the world of love, I found a citizen of the world of love. Then I lost that experience and you know how love makes for a good life. I bought a return ticket into yours and now I don't see myself leaving you. Can you see how hypnotizing your love is my beautiful wife, my soulmate, my joy, my wife

89

Donna Andersen?

Me: I feel the same way about you, Mr. Andersen. I cannot not imagine my life without you now

Erick: I love you and me together, Left right left, we are taking it one step at a time, until we get all that love we give, I love us, I do.

Me: I do too, babe

Erick: Your love is beyond my imagination. This feeling is high, this is love untold. The streaks are impeccable and I wish they were foretold. Hey, just don't kill me with your love. Kisses, Mwah!

Me: That is so sweet, babe

Erick: Your love is my everyday food. This love is delicious and is this your way of making me salivate all my life? Just came to say I love you!

Me: You are the sweetest man in the world hands down

Erick: You always make my day, my nights have been sweet since a lady angel started making My days worthwhile. You're more than sweet, my love

Me: Let me know when you want to walk me through that bitcoin purchase either today or tomorrow is fine with me. I am home and will be home tomorrow too, Ok?

Erick: Can you download an app called Blockchain and Coinbase on your phone?

Me: Blockchain wallet?

Erick: Blockchain is a app, my love. Go to the app store and download it.

Me: Ok, give me a few minutes to download them. I found them in the app store, babe. I am downloading both apps

Erick: Yeah honey, you are a good girl! Now sign up for both carefully ok honey? We are going to use Blockchain first, my love.

Me: Ok, walk me through the process, I just set them both up.

Erick: Alright my love log into your bitcoin, you have your

wallet set up now?
Me: Yes, do I fill in the request for $1000?
Erick: Honey, onto the left of the blockchain app you will see buy or sell sign. Type in the amount and it will show you the bitcoin equivalent, can you do that?
Me: There is no buy or sell and request asks me to send via message or mail?
Erick: Ok, go on the Coinbase app and you should see a platform to buy bitcoin. Once you see a platform to buy from your card then we can proceed.

He sent me two videos. The first was "Buy Bitcoin Instantly with your Blockchain Wallet." The other was "How to Buy Bitcoin in Coinbase"; both are YouTube videos. Blockchain is a digital currency platform app, and so is Coinbase. They operate differently. Blockchain you buy bitcoin on a separate platform and transfer to the app, but Coinbase you can buy and sell on the app, and it is easier to maneuver within the app, especially for a first-time user. Blockchain also means a digital database containing information (such as records of financial transactions) that can be simultaneously used and shared within a large decentralized network. The technology at the heart of bitcoin and other virtual currencies. Blockchain is an open, distributed ledger that can record transactions between two parties efficiently and in a verifiable and permanent way: this information is provided by Webster's Dictionary.

Me: I bought the bitcoin through Coinbase $1000 worth, babe
Erick: Very smart girl, now I need you to send the bitcoin to this wallet ID from Coinbase 1QDHe4mCg2PNJe-BAtFCGbX5tfed1CyK9Uq this is the wallet ID you need to type in, can you do that?

(Another YouTube video named "How to Send Bitcoin" he sent me to assist me.)

Me: I sent it to the wallet address recommended in Coinbase.

Erick: Did you send it to the wallet ID I gave you? The wallet ID is used to move the bitcoin from one person to another or to a company that accepts it as payment. The are usually only used once per transaction and once sent they cannot be retrieved!

Me: It gave me a different wallet ID to transfer to! I am so confused with this!

Erick: My love, what did you do? I posted some videos for you. You should not be confused and I did post the wallet ID for you to send the bitcoin to. That is all that is remaining if you followed my instructions.

Me: Ok, it told me to send it to wallet ID in my app. I do not have any idea how to send it to your wallet ID? I copied your ID but do not know how to utilize it in the app?

Erick: My love, did you watch the video tutorials I sent you?

Me: Yes, but it did not pertain to this particular app and you cannot drag and drop the wallet ID on the app.

Erick: Babe, In the dashboard can you see account? Can you take a picture of your dashboard? when it asked you to send to your wallet ID, you should of have placed it in the wallet ID that I gave you.

I copied and posted four screen shots of various transactions in my Coinbase app and sent it to him. I assumed he would know how to maneuver around through this app and how to securely advise me so this transaction would go smoother. Instead, he sent me YouTube videos to teach myself how to complete the transaction. I thought he was the financial expert and consultant to breeze through these apps. I know realize these videos is how he learned, and possibly by trial and error.

Erick: Do you see the airplane sign on the top right side where you see BTC?

Me: Yes I do the last screen is what popped up and then the BTC wallet address.

Erick: Look at the this one the second screen that you sent

Scammed in America

me. See the airplane sign on the Top where BTC is just click on that airplane sign, do you see it on the far right?
Me: Here is a copy of the current screen, what does this mean?
Erick: It means that you have to visit the support to verify some steps for your own interest OK? But you are doing great, my love. Visit the support now, honey.
Me: OK, I thought I lost the money! When I contacted support page it told me section by section what to expect regarding the balance on the account.

(I screenshot what support had sent me and posted a copy to him to see.)

Me: It says the bitcoin is on hold for 5 days for verifying funds from my bank account to Coinbase.
Erick: Alright my love. You are a great learner and I am proud of you, OK?
Me: Ok, when it clears the hold time, how do I send it to your wallet ID? I copied a picture of your Wallet ID but I will need you to verbally walk me through the process using this app, babe.
Erick: That is not a problem my wife. I am proud of you, honey. My Donna, you are my queen. Has eating and food ever been a source of tension and stress in a relationship? Has there ever been a factor in the breakup of a relationship?
Me: Erick, what are you talking about? Eating food should not be a source of tension or stress. Are you referring to stress eating? Or not having enough food to eat are the only reasons why eating food should lead to stressful situations, babe.

He did not answer my question; instead, he sent me twenty pictures on him on vacation with his late wife and children.

Erick: These are part of our last holiday together as family, honey. I am trying to give you an ideal of the man I am and

I enjoy spending time with my family now you are my family and I want you to know that we are going to create new beautiful memories together and that I promise you!

Me: I hope so too, babe because I am looking forward to making beautiful memories together with you in this new chapter in life. I am also looking forward to learning where you came from and the culture you were born with and hoping to also share my culture of where I was born into and customs. I am looking forward to our adventurous spirits and our wonderful life ahead.

Erick: No woman I have ever been with has ever said such sweet words to me, honey.

Me: That is how much I love you and I will remind you everyday, Mr. Andersen.

Erick: Thank you my love. Do you have a best friend, honey?

Me: I have several friends that I am close to, babe

Erick: Are there any single friends?

Me: Yes, I have a few single girlfriends

Erick: Oh, nice honey is any of them seeking a man? I have some trusted colleagues that are single.

Me: I do not know babe

Erick: Alright beautiful as long as we can make an effort to make happy homes, we will do all we can. Ask your friends what type of man she desires, age, height and all so that I can look through my single colleagues.

Me: Maybe we should wait until they attend our wedding and they can make their own matches.

Erick: I will give praise to heaven that I found you because you are sent from above to fill my heart with joy and from everything you do I know that I have found the angel that is signed to walk my destiny with me and I am looking forward to bring you into my world and proudly introduce you to everyone and vow my endless commitment to you my queen.

Me: I am so thankful to have such a beautiful soulmate in my

life to cherish every day in life.
Erick: How did you sleep my wife?
Me: Like a baby, how did you sleep my love
Erick: I'm perfectly made my love and what more can I ask for but to wake up knowing that I will be enjoying sweet feeling of love from you my love.
Me: You are perfectly made for me, Erick Andersen

By now we have been corresponding for three weeks and I have invested one thousand dollars, and we were getting married and I was moving in with him. It is well known the scammers work with a plan to quickly get their victim's trust and handing over of their money within weeks of meeting. This scammer used investing to lure me to give up my money, but later, things changed, as you will see. Each scammer works differently, but the scheme is all the same. To move in fast, lure their victim to trust them, then use their good hearts to give up money.

Erick: I will not ever put you in the position to be sad my love because that will mean that I don't love myself. I am gradually getting ready for your arrival, my wife.
Me: That is sweet, babe
Erick: I miss you and I wanted to tell you that you are always on my mind. I wanted to let you know That I want to take you to the alter and pledge my lifelong commitment to loving only you, my queen Donna Andersen!
Me: You are a sweetheart and I cannot wait to be your wife and to start this magical journey together.
Erick: I believe you my love and I feel complete and fulfilled because what I set out for to find on internet dating and I found even more than I had hoped for.
Me: You are a beautiful soul and a godsend to me and my heart is full because of you. I will love and adore you for the rest of my life, Erick Andersen!
Erick: You know there comes in life where everything seems like a movie or should I say too good to be true but you re-

member that there is a time and season for everything and when the time is right it is smooth and natural and this is the way I feel about us.

Me: I believe if you are honest and live a good life then god makes sure and you are looked after and in my lifetime I could have left this earth several times but god had other plans for me. I have an endless capacity to love another just as most people do. I am so glad he allowed us to cross paths in this lifetime and I cannot wait to see what he has in store for us.

Erick: It can only get better and who else would I ever hope and pray to enjoy this phase of my life after years of pain but with a woman that believes in me and that is a great motivation for any man. Your time to be celebrated is now my love.

Me: I wanted to share with you a beautiful card that my father sent my mother when he was away during WWII in the army. It was a Christmas card.

Erick: That is wonderful are you bringing it with you when you come, I hope. I just forwarded it to my mom and she said it just brought back memories of her and my dad who also served during the war.

Me: I cannot wait to meet her she is a precious woman and I have a soft spot for mothers who have influenced their children with their hearts and love.

Erick: Oh really, then you know that you have found a man fully groomed by a woman's heart of gold. God gave you favor and grace, my beauty

Me: Are you ready for your trip to Miami tomorrow?

Erick: Yes, my love I am flying with some of my team.

Me: Take a lot of pictures for me and I wish you a safe trip and god speed, my love.

Erick: I will my love and will call to get a kiss

Me: I definitely cannot wait to see your face and hear your voice, babe. What time is your flight?

Erick: We will be flying private by 11 A.M.

Me: How long does it take from there to Miami?

Erick: It takes almost 4 hours, my love

Me: Wow, that is good time because from here in Detroit it takes 2-1/2 hours.

Erick: Yeah babe tops is 5 hours before we land once take off. Have you flown private before my queen?

Me: No, I have only flown commercial both large and small planes.

Erick: Alright my love I will call you and make some videos with my team for you my love.

Me: I will be looking forward to seeing your face and the team videos

Erick: Thank you my love. I am glad I didn't trade you for another and I am glad I did not propose to another and I am also glad it did not take forever to find you when I signed up for Zoosk. now I am excited and my heart is filled with joy and looking forward to the day I will officially vow to make you my one and only. I love you my darling wife and destiny helper, Mrs. Donna Andersen.

Me: That is so sweet, babe! I am glad to have met you on Zoosk especially when I was getting disgusted with the app and when it asked me to look outside my area is when I met you. I am so glad I clicked on your profile and took a chance. I hope we have a beautiful future together and I cannot wait to start our life together.

Erick: My love for you will last longer than eternity. That is why I am not afraid to spend forever in your arms.

Me: I cannot wait to finally meet and be in your arms, Mr. Andersen

Erick: Just so you know nothing can separate you from my love. As the stars are in the sky, so are you to me, as the moon is to dark, so am I to you I love you my queen, my angel.

Me: I love you to the moon and back, too

Erick: I want you to know that all my vows to you I will keep and every kiss I give is an expression of my love for you. I cannot wait for our wedding night, I love you

Me: I cannot wait either my love and I am looking forward to being your wife

Erick: My precious woman it feels so good to awake knowing I will enjoy the beauty of being loved by you an awesome, humble, pure, beautiful, sexy, caring and God loving woman like you as my heart keeper and destiny helper, God bless you Mrs. Donna Andersen

Me: Thank you, Mr. Andersen

Erick: Alright my love I will be leaving soon, I will miss you my love.

Me: I am looking forward to video chatting with you because it will be the highlight of my day

Erick: Yes, I am looking forward to it also, my love. I want your spirit to be with me beautiful

Me: My love and spirit is always with your, Erick

Erick: This is the first time in a while I wish I was traveling for business with my wife and I know soon you and I will be traveling together to handle business so you can see first hand how I work and to also hold my hand and kiss me when I perform exceptionally well and I know you understand what I mean honey.

Me: Yes, I do understand and I cannot wait to travel with you and be by your side and learn about your business I will be your biggest fan, babe

Several hours later I received several videos: the first was of his suitcases and feet, then him and several individuals loading onto a private jet and then one of the pilot in the cockpit and, last, of him and others drinking and toasting on the plane. There was sound to all the videos, and the last one, they were toasting to a successful trip. There was a video call several minutes after the last video. I heard noise, and it was hard to talk, so the video call was very brief. Five hours later, there were pictures sent of him and four other men outside the plane and him by himself as if he had arrived at his destination.

Erick: I miss you love

Me: Love your outfit, you look so handsome

Erick: My love, thank you for your sweet compliment

Me: Are you settled in yet? I miss talking to you today you are my beautiful soul

Erick: Yes, my love I am settled in and I miss you also, How are you my love?

Me: I am at work now getting ready for a busy night ahead. I have some business to take care of tomorrow but everything seems to be moving along good. How is the weather down there? Is it warm?

Erick: I miss you a lot and yeah it is warm here and I am getting ready to be with you also, babe I am excited and one of your values is optimism and that's adorable and that is a trait I want by my side.

Me: I can handle anything as long as the end goal is to be with you the rest of my life.

Erick: And you know that I Erick chose you and I cannot see a life alone anymore without you and with you anything is possible, my wife.

Me: I feel the same about you, Mr. Andersen

Erick: You are my gift from God our creator that was sent to be my destiny helper to accomplish what he has destined for us to do and I will do my best to cherish you

(A picture of him sitting in what appears to be a kitchen in the background was sent.)

Me: What a handsome face you have, Mr. Andersen

Erick: Thank you, I can picture you sitting on my lap and kissing me, my love

Me: I cannot wait to kiss you everyday of our life together and we are going to be in the same time zone now, babe

Erick: Honey as long as your mind is ready that is all that matters. I know the best of you is to begin to manifest and I

will do my best to bring it all out.
Me: You definitely will and I have no doubt whatsoever and I will be prepared for an abundance of laughter too.
Erick: Thank you my love for your sincere assurance. My love do you love to read?
Me: Yes, I do I have read books most of my life.
Erick: That's great and you really are a smart girl

(He sent me two more pictures of him standing in front of others giving what looked like a presentation.)

Erick: My love, I am just finishing the first session then next free lunch then a question and answer session for today.
Me: I will have to put in for an early termination of my lease on my apartment and pay $1830 to get out of it.
Erick: Alright my love, I hope you can handle this? I am proud of you and if you need my assistance in any way my wife please do not hesitate to mention ok?
Me: All I need is a date when you are coming to get me because my last day will be May 10, 2019 and I figure it will take me a week to wrap up loose ties here and then the rest is up to you.
Erick: Alright my precious I have no reason to allow you to stay there after your last day at work from now let us begin to pray about it I will come the weekend after your last day at work so that we can have a week there to see everyone and do the things we have to do.
Me: Sounds good to me I pray everyday things stay on track till you arrive.
Erick: Yes, babe we will keep our faith and keep doing what you are doing and do not give in to any negativity because this is a big step for the both of us and we must always remember we made the choice and in we are mature enough to make the right choices and I am in love with the woman you are and I know that my heart has found a home in you.

Me: Listen there is no negativity just positivity here. I am excited about the choices I have made to be with you for the rest of my life. It is your love that will help me make it through any obstacles in life and I thank god for you everyday.
Erick: My love is yours because I would not change my choice of choosing you because of the excitement I need as a man when I think of my woman is even more when I think of us together.
Me: That is why I love you my beloved Erick
Erick: I am excited about this new life my beautiful wife.

It is known by those who study these scammers that they work with a scripted storyline. I know going over these letters and texts that I can tell when he would go off script. First, all the notes and letters of love were perfectly spelled and well written; then when he had to wing it on his own, the wording was strange and misspelled to the point I would ask "What are you talking about? and "What do you mean?" Sometimes he would not answer my questions right away or not at all, actually not answering at all. Two more pictures were sent again in seminar mode.

Me: Wow, awesome pictures! Is that you in the yellow tie?
Erick: Yes, my love I know in a time not too far from now you and I will be together my love and doing things we love to do together.
Me: I know and I miss you too.
Erick: My queen, you now know that my life is no longer single.
Me: I hope so because I no longer feel single anymore
Erick: I love you my darling wife. You know that is how our creator has made our path. My colleagues say you have an amazing smile.
Me: Tell them its because of you that I smile constantly
Erick: Thank you my love, you know I was proud looking at you. Did you have dinner honey?

Me: Yes, I ate before work my love, did you eat?
Erick: What did you have my love?
Me: Chef Salad
Erick: Ok my love, I missed you today. There is a light that shines in your path and that light is one I called forth in my world when I was asking from my creator to send forth my destiny helper into my world and I know that when you came I saw you in my vision and now that I have found you I will always give glory to my creator for sending you my way love.
Me: Aww, I love you my soulmate
Erick: I will do my best to also take care of you and bring out the best of you so that you can also give praises to your creator for bringing me into your world also to fulfill everything you have ever prayed for in a man that you will spend the rest of your life with my Queen Donna Andersen and I cannot wait for the day I will walk you to the alter and pledge my everlasting commitments to loving you and bringing the best of you as long as you are willing to keep trusting me to lead us to our expectations of heart desires and our love ones also and the people our creator has predestined us to fulfill and I know you understand what I mean, my love.
Me: Yes I understand everything you say babe. I promise to always have faith and unconditional love for you because you are my destiny and my soulmate and I know god crossed our paths for a reason and you are more than I could ever wish for a partner in this lifetime.
Erick: May all praises belong to him as we fulfill our calling on our lives.
Me: Amen!
Erick: How was work today, my love?
Me: Good I tried to stay busy and keep my mind busy with business. The contractors are disappointed that I will be retiring and they do not like change very well but a girl has to do what she has to for love.
Erick: When my late wife passed away I was devastated but

I realized that it is my choice to know that everything happens for a reason and the reason I still continue to live is not because I am better than her but because destiny needs her to watch over me and the boys and while mine is also a vessel to show and share true love with a woman like you because you are also an angel and I am a born destiny angel keeper and lover and you deserve to be loved by a man like me. Have you told your niece about me and to do a photo shoot for us, my love?

Me: Of course I told her and I asked her to do our engagement photos. She is just starting out but she does beautiful photos and when we decide on when and where to take then we can make arrangements for her to come with us.

Erick: Have you ever cheated sexually on your past relationship before my love? And if yes what happened?

Me: No, I have always been loyal to whomever I have been in a relationship with even when my ex was suspected of cheating on me. I don't believe in revenge sex and if I pledged my loyalty to you I remain loyal.

Erick: All because I'm the man destined for you. I kneel beside you here today, I kneel beside you and I pray, That its you, its only you who will share my tomorrows and yesterdays. I searched a lifetime and found you a bridge to forever I share with you. Open your heart and let me in as I give you this promise of love. I heard an angel saying your name. Now I know the world is not the same. A little heaven is what you are as we with a love of a thousand dreams not so far and may the blessings of our lord above. his light will guide us with a love for you and me forever more as I give you this promise of love. Now that I have you for my own, as god is our witness never let me go and feel the love grow as we become one. One hand, one heart and we are one soul and as I stand before you as just a man and I need your help to understand of what is life without you as I promise you this day and forever this promise of love.

Me: I promise to love you always and to make you the happiest man possible. I will stand with you side by side before god and pledge my heart to you before god in whatever endeavor he has in store for us. I have no doubt that we were meant for each other and I am so looking forward to our future. I love you forever, Mr. Erick Andersen and I promise my love to you for eternity.

Erick: My love I also want to make you my beneficiary in everything that has to do with me because I know that if anything should happen which I don't hope for I know that you will see that our families get to the destination we both have wished and prayed for.

Me: I will abide by whatever you wish and pray I never lose you because I could never imagine life without you my love. You own half of my heart and soul and I do not know if my heart would ever heal if I lost you.

Erick: I love you baby! Have you gotten approval for the bitcoin transaction, my love?

Me: I received a message that it was approved but when I checked the app it said the funds were on hold for 16 days from March 23rd. They said it was for fraud protection.

Erick: I think they will show you a place to also contact the support system, my love

Me: That is where I got the information from. They said they placed the initial deposit on hold for security reasons and I cannot lift the hold before its time. The money was withdrawn from my bank account so the money is secured. When they lift the hold I will need to know how to transfer it to the wallet you gave me.

Erick: Alright my love. You know you learn very fast. I have no problems with your learning skills

Me: This gives me time to learn to maneuver within the app too. I love learning new things especially when it pertains to our future.

Erick: That is good my love. I admire that aspect about you.

> **Me:** I am always curious about things in life and I ask a lot of questions.
> **Erick:** I am also curious and I understand when a person is my love just ask me anything!
> **Me:** I will definitely ask you a lot of questions that is a given and I am not shy to ask. I cannot wait to pick your beautiful mind, my love
> **Erick:** Thank you my love and I know you and I have a path with destiny.
> **Me:** Can I ask you a simple question? Before you rest that beautiful mind? I need you to clarify The address as 401b Ville Dr. or just 401 Ville Dr.?
> **Erick:** Yes, my love 401b Ville Dr.

I Google searched this address and the other three addresses he gave me. This address showed a small park, and when I tried to do a change of address, it would not accept it. The United States Postal Service uses Google to verify addresses as a mail address, and they could never confirm this address. Every single piece of mail I had sent was returned to sender, as no such address exists. The other two addresses did exist, but one he claimed as a residence was a small office, and the other was the same. I never had any mail sent to the other addresses. This should have been a major red flag, but I seemed to give him the benefit of the doubt about the situation.

> **Erick:** My queen, my wife and beautiful partner we are going to have an amazing jointing.

Another picture of him with several other men I assumed were his associates he worked with. He was still in Miami, according to him, and it was a work trip for his business. He worked as a financial specialist, so I just assumed he was training others on how to financially invest their money, whether for business or personal portfolio.

> **Me:** How was your day, my love
> **Erick:** Going productive babe. How is yours beautiful?

Me: So far so good and I pray it continues as such
Erick: Alright my love, How is your health? Are you looking after yourself now for me?
Me: Of course, I am good. My health is fine and I am taking a break from working so hard.
Erick: Alright my wife! I am glad because health is also our priorities in our home my love and I am proud of you honey.
Me: How are you doing my handsome love?
Erick: I'm glowing with pride because I have found what I am looking for. I know you are a fruitful soul and any seed sown in you will give fruits so I consider myself a blessed man.
Me: I am very blessed to have met you and am looking forward to the beautiful future ahead.
Erick: Given the choice of anyone around the world, whom would you want as a dinner guest?
Me: Bill Gates would be my first pick and not for his money but because he is a staunch Humanitarian and philanthropist!
Erick: That is cute my love, you never know.

I realize now he had no idea who Bill Gates was, but I thought I was talking to an businessman who resided in America, not a foreign man who probably has never stepped foot in the United States. I am almost positive the only thing he has to do with business in America is scamming unsuspecting women!

Erick: What song do you sing to most?
Me: It changes all the time but I like Shine by Collective Soul
Erick: Interesting honey, I love singing in the shower my love
Me: What do you sing? What is your favorite song to sing?
Erick: Songs of praises, honey
Me: Can you sing Amazing Grace?
Erick: Yes, My love though not all the stanza. Sometimes songs just play in my head. I will sing for you someday.
Erick: Would you like to be famous? If yes in what way?

Me: No, I have never strived to be famous nor have I ever craved fame. I am an introvert and most introverts are quiet and reserved and excel well in smaller intimate groups. I like to be the best version of me and really don't care about what others think of me. There are plenty of famous introverts but none of them like the notoriety.
Erick: You are the type that loves to be the brain behind the star and you derive joy to see what you are involved to excel.
Me: You are correct with that assumption. I never craved the limelight but if someone else shines in it I would have no problem helping them attain their goals.
Erick: If you were able to live to the age of 90 and retain either the mind or the body of a 30 year old for the last 60 years of your life which would you choose?
Me: Definitely the mind! The body can be fixed but if you lose the mind it is gone for good.
Erick: You are a smart woman! I am proud of you. Do you have a secret hunch about how you will die?
Me: No, and very few people who have walked this earth do have premonitions regarding the end of their life. Do you have premonitions?
Erick: Yes, baby to have my love ones beside me and to sing hymns with me to send me home.

During our conversations, I realized he said one thing and meant another thing. It did confuse me, but keep in mind, he claimed to be from The Bahamas, and me not being familiar with Bahamian culture, it would confuse me, but I accepted it for this reason. Had he been an American, I would have questioned his quirks.

Erick: Name threes things you and me as partners appear to have in common?
Me: Patience, Humbled and Grace, my love
Erick: You are indeed my wife, It means we are a perfect match. For what in life do you feel most grateful for?

Me: For life itself and the ability to love

Erick: Wise woman

Me: What are you most grateful for, babe?

Erick: I am grateful for life, my family and you. What is your greatest accomplishment of your life?

Me: Overcoming adversity and meeting you. But I feel my greatest accomplishment is still yet to come.

Erick: I love you baby! Back to a busy morning Another picture of him and three other men standing next to a small jet.

Erick: I just received this, my love. One of my team took this photo

Me: Nice photo, babe

Erick: Thank you, my love. You will soon meet all of them. I miss you

Me: I received my new passport in the mail today, babe

Erick: Well I know that I wished for a spell that will last for a lifetime because I have been victim of such spell and I know how amazing it is to be under that spell so I give myself willingly to be your victim of your spell. You look beautiful my love and I am proud of you.

Me: I am working hard to make things happen so we can be together permanently and I am hoping there will be no glitches from here on out.

Erick: Praise God, my angel. You are working hard and I am impressed my love. Have you been called a workaholic?

Me: I have a good work ethnic and always have. I strive to be the best of myself everyday. most people are competitive against others but I am against myself to be better at what ever I do everyday. So I do consider myself to be a driven woman but it can come with consequences too.

Erick: What are the consequences, my love.

Me: You sometimes get lost in what your ultimate goal is and work to hard as life sometimes pass you by.

Erick: Why I am not surprised? Only a well rounded person thinks this way Do you have anything you have in mind that you have left to accomplish?

Me: I have a list of things I would love to accomplish to do in life. I do not look back I look forward in life to the future.

Erick: That is very true my love. I got a hard on thinking of you today.

Me: That is sweet, babe

Erick: I am serious my love. You know what I was thinking about?

Me: What my love?

Erick: I could see you and I in our private yacht apartment. Having a romantic night with wine and holding hands and enjoying the natural peace of the ocean.

Me: That is a beautiful scenario. I think that is a attainable goal, babe

Erick: Have I told you about the global ship apartments?

Me: Yes, we have discussed this in earlier conversations.

Erick: That's good! My birthday is coming up and so is yours and we need to plan how we can make them memorable.

Me: Everyday with you will be memorable but special occasions will be exceptional. What would you like to do for your birthday in June, my love?

Erick: Yes, and yours is October 17th my love

Me: Think about it and let me know what you would love to do to celebrate your birthday this year and I will accommodate whatever you require to do. Your happiness is a priority, babe

Erick: I think getting an apartment in the ship will be a good birthday present and go on a mission to render love to devastated countries.

Me: I love those ideas and will do what is possible to make those things happen.

Erick: Thank you my love. What would you want for yours?

Me: All I want is to spend some quality time with you and if giving back to those in need and us working side by side is part of the gift that keeps on giving, Mr. Andersen

Erick: I love you my queen Donna Andersen. Do you have any knowledge of interior design?

Me: Yes, my love. I love to decorate within my home. I have a creative side too.

Erick: I know you do, my love. I am thinking we can redecorate the house when you come

Me: I would love that, my soulmate

Erick: You know that when your dad had sex with your mom there were a million chances for other lives to have breathed but destiny chose you. Not to come live in a blank world but a path that has specifically been carved for you and this path that has been chosen for you required us to cross such paths and I have opened my world up to be used as a vessel to fulfill your hearts desire to be wholeheartedly loved completely by a man completing you.

Me: Erick Andersen I have been missing you for a long time in my life. I have no doubt you are my completeness. I have faith we will lead a extraordinary life together.

Erick: Yes, we are one my wife. You are not dreaming I am here with you now and forever. I am not going away but to the right destiny together. Thank you for choosing me, my love

Me: You are a beautiful soul, Mr. Andersen

Erick: I am fulfilled already as I have you in my life. You are the source of all sweetness to me. I love you more than you can imagine.

Me: Awww, you melt my heart babe. I love and adore you more everyday.

(Another picture of him with two other men with a wine-decanter-filled wall in the background.)

Me: You look handsome my love

Erick: Thank you my wife

Me: Was that a wine tasting? It looks awesome

Erick: A wine lodge, my love. Change is constant in life, very true but I don't ever want to change from you. You are the best gift from life to me. I look forward to every new day as it gives me more reason to love you more. I can never get over you and I do not even want to.

Me: Everyday my love grows stronger and stronger. You are my one and only and never forget that, my love

Erick: Over and over I fall for you. What would my life be without you in it? You complete me baby. You have captured my mind, heart, body and soul. I do not even want this feeling to end as it gives me thorough happiness. You came into my life and gave me more joy. You came into my heart and made it your home. You are my priceless gem and I love you so much.

I think the main reason these scammers are so successful is the fact they do their homework and perfect their skills so that they educate themselves on what a woman wants to hear. The poems and even YouTube songs of love is the key to their success. All women want to be told they are beautiful and loved and perfect for their partner. "How are you?" "Are you okay?" "I love you," and even "Have you been taken care of yourself?" These are all common questions each and every scammer asks their victim. They constantly proclaim their love and dedication to their victims. It is known that the most successful ones know what to say and when to say it fluidly. They learn from one "client" to another what works and what doesn't. Each and every victim of this scam will tell you no other man made them feel the way these scammers did before the money came into play. For all being said, they are professional at the art of deception of making you believe you are the one strictly for them and you become their world. I truly believe that my scammer had victimized a lot of women. He was definitely very good and heavily invested in his scams. But most of us victims who have done their homework on these scammers realize just how dangerous they are, because they work within a network, and what some of us realize is we are being scammed by more than one scammer. They ask questions, and your answers are passed from one scammer to another. It is common to be scammed by more than one scammer simultaneously. One scammer picks up the storyline where another leaves off. This often happens when there is a bigger payout involved. They first story I read of Romance Scammers was exactly of this type of scam. They made off with two million dollars of the victim's money, and she ended her life. That is why I speak up and always will for myself and other victims, because it causes so much damage to its victims psychologically.

> **Me:** I love you so much my soul is at peace. I fall asleep dreaming of you and awake wanting you.
> **Erick:** Ever since I met you, my dreams have always been so amazing. You are always there to hold me and make me fly high. You are the light that brightens up my days and the moon that watches me at night. I trust you and I will make sure are always happy with you my love and grace.
> **Me:** I will make it a priority to put our happiness above all else. I trust you with my heart, body and soul forever, my love
> **Erick:** Baby, if you still love to drive when we are living together there are cars here for you to Drive. If you want a new one, I will be honored to buy one for you. If you still feel the need your car I can't say otherwise. On the other hand, I can still advise you to sell it and invest the money while you and I build on our future so that I will always remind you the wise decisions you make the last phase of your single hood.
> **Me:** I was thinking of leaving it with my brother to try to sell it for me it is in good condition and well maintenance
> **Erick:** That's not a bad idea my love. We will keep praying for the best decision OK? **Me:** Yes, my love I just wanted your opinion on the matter.
> **Erick:** Ok love, that shows how much you value my opinion and I cherish that honey. I think it is also good when you see the wind of change, you give it full room to take effect. If you put your car up for sale how much do you think you can sell it for my love?
> **Me:** I am checking the blue book price to see what it is worth
> **Erick:** Alright my wife, get back to me on that my wife. Have you collected the hard copy of your passport?
> **Me:** Yes, I received it yesterday

ScamHaters United just posted on their Facebook page: "When They

Have Your Phone Number." They received a comment on why it is a problem them having your phone number. They can use your phone number, email address to hack into your PayPal account and launder money. This has happened to victims. They do not need your sign-in or password to hack into an account. They can find out your provider with email address and clone the SIM. They will try and continue contact with you even after you disconnect from them; do not engage. I have personally had numerous attempts on my bank account and PayPal account. My scammer, Erick, had my phone number, email address also. I constantly monitor my accounts and changed my bank and email accounts for my protection. You must look at it as possible identity theft because of what they know and have access to.

Erick: Congratulations baby girl, we are ready to take on the world. That is how everything about your new family is in your knowledge my love. You are everything I want from a woman.
Me: I am so excited for our future together, Mr. Andersen
Erick: My love what are you doing?
Me: Laying in my bed resting, babe
Erick: I'm back to work my love and I miss you. I am expecting Zeus tomorrow morning.
Me: I bet she misses you and I miss and love you too.
Erick: Yes, my love I do too. This should be my last trip alone without you.
Me: The next one should be when you come to get me, babe
Erick: Yes love, and then we can travel together everywhere we go.
Me: I cannot wait to be with you the rest of my life and traveling together.
Erick: I'm looking forward to that with excitement, Mrs. Andersen. Thank you for making everyday amazing. Our destiny is to be together in matrimony and I have already started telling some of my associates, my love
Me: That is sweet babe! I cannot wait to meet your family and friends.

Erick: I cannot wait to introduce you to them too. Today is more about networking between delegates, my love.
Me: How are you today my happy soul?
Erick: My love yes I am always happy. You know that I am committed to living with you as long as I live.
Me: I have no doubt what so ever, babe

(Another picture of him with four other men came across.)

Me: Looks like fun
Erick: Yes, my love I miss you and I told them they should pose for my queen. You know when I came home I felt your presence. It was like you was opening the door for me and welcoming me with a kiss.
Me: That is because I am always with you in your heart.
Erick: And Yes, I am always feeling your presence, my beautiful wife I have sent an email of intent to purchase one of the apartments in the ship.
Me: Really?
Erick: Yes, my wife I have started. You inspire me to carve an amazing life for us.
Me: That is beautiful, Mr. Andersen
Erick: My love there is so many ideas I will love us to be sharing with each other and if you have any ideas feel free to share with me just as I am going to share with you.
Me: I will my love, I know what a beautiful mind you have and I cannot wait to collaborate with you.
Erick: That reminds me babe, when will you complete the bitcoin transaction for your spot?
Me: I checked yesterday and the hold will not be lifted for 12 more days. I figure by April 11th I was also able to get step by step info on how to transfer to your wallet.
Erick: That is right my baby! I am proud of you and I want us to travel together for business also.
Me: I will follow you to the moon and back whether it be for

business or pleasure
Erick: Thank you my love. Do you believe in spanking a child? What type of discipline do you believe in (time-out, standing in the corner, taking away privileges, etc.)?
Me: I think it depends on the child, each child should be considered different when it comes to discipline. Some kids talking to works for them to see how they failed, some require limiting privileges. I do not believe in physically disciplining any child. Spanking does not work on any child.
Erick: Thank you for telling me your opinion, my love. I have always engaged in a word discipline and I am open to also welcome your own view on how we make our younger generations either equipped to be the better version of us. One of the great strength is your genuine love for the will of our creator to be accomplished through our generations and that is also why I know I can rest our vision in your bosom.
Me: You are welcome, my love
Erick: You look beautiful my darling and you are my shining wife. What is your favorite time of day to be intimate?

Some of these questions he asked came out of the blue. I wondered if they read *Cosmopolitan*, the magazine, because these are not really the type of questions a young man from Nigeria would ask a woman. You be the judge! I assumed he asked them to get an idea of our compatibility; instead, it was to gain my trust for manipulation.

Me: Evening is my favorite time to be intimate, babe
Erick: What do you think we need to work on the most in our relationship?
Me: Spending more time together and getting to know one another better
Erick: And you can be assured that this man loves you with all his heart, my love. I will never tire of telling you that before we go to bed and every new morning, my darling
Me: I will not ever tire in reminding you just how much you

are loved in return, babe
Erick: I cannot stop looking at your picture my beauty. This new hair sits like a crown on you and it gave you a new look.
Me: I needed a new look for my new life with you my love. I am glad you approve.
Erick: You know you look like a super model. I have always told you this honey. What is going on in your mind, my love
Me: I am so blessed to have you in my life. I loved hearing your voice today it made my day so much brighter.
Erick: I'm proud of the things you have accomplished today it shows how organized you are
Me: I have to stay organized it will be 4 weeks and I am all your 24/7. What are you doing my beautiful husband.
Erick: I was reading a blog and responding to some e-mail baby. I am chatting up my Mom and making plans for the two boys summer stay.

According to Erick, his two boys, Mark and Logan, were in school in New York, where his brother lives. Because he travels for business a lot, it is easier to have them with his brother instead of with him. He claims the boys went to his mom's place for holidays and spent in The Bahamas. It was weird thinking why the boys do not stay with him and just get a nanny, because he mentioned having a gardener and housekeeping where he lived in Boulder City.

Me: That is awesome I bet she cannot wait to spend time with them.
Erick: Yes, baby and I am looking forward for you to meet her. Have you ever been a host before?
Me: Party Host? Of course I have hosted many functions. Birthday parties, Receptions, Baby Showers BBQ's and Memorial Dinners is that the kind of hosting you were referring to?
Erick: Thank you, my love. Believe me she is looking forward to meet you too. I want to ask you How would you feel to be made part of my board of directors for my company?
Me: How ever I can assist you I am all in.

Erick: I just sent a message to my lawyer as well my love. He will get back to me as well. We might open a branch in your city to incorporate any family members with brains that might be willing to be involved.

Me: I am willing to learn anything you are ready to teach me babe. I am all yours

Erick: You are an arrow in the hands of the right man this is what I always tell my boys and you are the sharpest arrow in the hands of this man. Do you know the procedure to register a company in your city?

Me: No, I do not babe

Erick: You should find out for us, my love Ok?

Me: Which city are you interested in Detroit? Or the surrounding suburbs?

Erick: Which city is a good corporation location?

Me: Detroit is a hard location the suburbs would be easier maybe Ann Arbor. I do not know what your company looks for in a corporate location.

Erick: Most important is the accessibility and the safety. I will need your assistance in helping us make inquiries on getting an office space there and how we can register a company in your city. What bank do you use, my love?

I now realize they must not have had a connection within this area. I do know there are elaborate organizations that they work with. My scammer was obviously a part of that organization. They set up dummy companies for money laundering and filtering other scams. It is known they are organized criminals; they have people all over the world and different scams and crimes to support their organization. I assumed Erick owned his own business and was a businessman, so I never question his intent, but once I realized it was all fake, I could not wrap my head around what exactly he was aiming for, but once I looked into Romance Scammers and how they work, it made sense that they would try to recruit smart women to assist them in their crime. Both of the other victims of Erick Andersen that I know of were also smart businesswomen too. So it makes ssense to try and recruit us for their scheme of crime.

Dorothy Harding

I know I have not committed a crime, and neither did one of the others, but I cannot speak for the third victim.

> **Me:** Bank of America but I will see what I can find out
> **Erick:** I will also begin to structure you to begin to receive some payments for us to gradually begin to build our account together, OK?
> **Me:** Ok, but I would like to know more about your company to do so.
> **Erick:** Honey would you also like a court wedding?
> **Me:** Court house wedding or courtyard wedding?
> **Erick:** No love like where we go to attorneys office to be legally married by him.
> **Me:** So, you want a office wedding by an attorney? No regular wedding or both?
> **Erick:** First our regular wedding then to legalize it by an attorney, my love **Me:** That is fine by me, babe
> **Erick:** I will need you to give me your full information down in case I will need you to receive A payment on our behalf ok?
> **Me:** What exact information do you need?
> **Erick:** Bank information and information for our company registration. And would you be interested for us to run a charity organization together, my love?
> **Me:** I would love to do a charity organization together. Do you want me to open a separate bank account for business?
> **Erick:** Yes babe, that will be when we register the company but for now while you make inquires I will just need the basic information of your account so I can have you receive some payments On my behalf ok my mighty arrow?
> **Me:** I will make the inquires and get you the necessary information. My account has been recently targeted with a fraud scam so it is heavily secured so that is out of the question.
> **Erick:** Alright my wife that is the first step to prove to our creator that we have decided to take a leap of faith to fulfill-

ment of our destinies. Many are called and few are chosen.

Right after I met Erick online, I had several hundred dollars debited from my checking account. The bank had caught it and put a freeze on my account until everything was resolved. They found that some scammers had gotten access to my debit card numbers and made a ninety-nine-cent purchase at a vending machine in Detroit that accepts credit cards before making a two-hundred-dollar purchase at a local department store. It was later cleared as an outside scam, and my money was returned, but it is a real hassle to work around in order to pay my bills with just my bank account and not my debit card. You have to be careful. I do not use my debit card frivolously, and I protect it at all times, but I still became a victim.

>**Erick:** Do you see a close friend or friends at least once a week? Do you speak to any of your friends on the phone every day?
>**Me:** No, not daily but I do see my friends at least several times weekly
>**Erick:** Alright my love, so you can be gone for long and won't cry over coming back to your friends?
>**Me:** No, I will miss them but will not cry over it. I am hoping to be so busy with my love of the life and starting this new chapter that I will not miss anything or anyone.
>**Erick:** One of the things on my bucket list is to travel the world with my significant half. So you are willing to travel the world with this man Erick as Mrs. Andersen?
>**Me:** Isn't that why I renewed my passport? I love to travel and cannot wait to be with the love of my life and travel abroad. I am looking forward to our next chapter together and being Mrs. Erick Andersen.
>**Erick:** Yes, my beautiful wife now you too understand me more and more and I love that. I will never let you down and I promise this is our destiny calling.

Another phone call came in it lasted two minutes. I started noticing that these calls were sporadic and were very short, always less than three minutes. He would claim bad reception or connection.

> **Erick:** Happy Mother's Day
> **Me:** Mother's Day??
> **Erick:** Yeah, it's an International Woman's Day I think my love
> **Me:** You're a sweetheart
> **Erick:** Thank you, beautiful. What are you doing?
> **Me:** Inquiring about the information you requested, business license has to be attained correct? To do business in Michigan
> **Erick:** You are my trusted arrow
> **Me:** What type of business are you looking at? What services are you looking to perform? These answers determine if state licenses permit is needed. City license is a separate entity.
> **Erick:** We are an investment and consulting company. We also sell and supply surgical hospital instruments.
> **Me:** When advising about investments you are to be licensed as an Investment Advisor per Department of Licensing and Regulatory Affairs. I find nothing regarding selling and supplying surgical instruments yet. That may be permit not license.

He sent me a page on his website peakcockbusinessgroup.com. Welcome, Peakcock Business Group is a leading highly diversified global investment company. We have access to a global array of traditional and non-traditional asset classes and provide sophisticated global investment strategies for institutional investors and public client investments and cash management strategies.

> **Me:** Is this the same name for both investments and selling medical supplies?
> **Erick:** I want us to have our own unique name. And this one will be just you and I. Something Like Eric Don Investment Group
> **Me:** Andersen Investment Group
> **Erick:** That is smart! You see one of the great potentials you have, You and I will be both signatory. You are a woman of

vision. That is a divine name!

I realize, had I actually started a business with him, I would have lost hundreds of thousands of dollars. He intended for me to attain loans and put money into accounts for him to attain. It was a ruse or set-up to access a lot of cash. Thank God logic ruled in my favor and I did not further look into obtaining a business license. He was knowledgeable about business enough to pursue me into looking into obtaining licensing and banking accounts for him to access to steal funds from.

>**Me:** How is Zeus? Was she excited to see you?
>**Erick:** Yes my queen, I will try to call you so both of us can say hello
>**Me:** I would love that besides I love hearing your voice, babe
>**Erick:** Oh, my love you are so sweet! Can I ask you for some information?
>**Me:** Yes, Erick you can what do you need?
>**Erick:** I need your banking information? Full bank details, bank address, swift code, routing number and your full name.
>**Me:** What do you need that information for?
>**Erick:** I am going to need this information to forward to my personal assistant to accept payments from some clients, Ok?
>**Me:** I do not know why but my bank will not accept payments electronically from unknown sources I do not give my personal banking info to anyone I do not know and besides it is only in my name. If we had a joint bank account it would be different, babe.
>**Erick:** Alright my love, we will look into changing that.

He never provided me with a reasonable excuse as to why he needed my personal banking info. I have talked to several others who did provide this information, and they had their accounts wiped out of all their funds, and some had money electronically deposited, then removed, and it was later discovered that the funds were being laundered from other victims of scams. It is well known that these scammers will ask for your personal information and run a credit report and attain credit under your name. You are a commodity to them, a source of constant income, nothing more!

Me: The bitcoin is ready for transfer as soon as you send me your wallet address and you will have to walk me through this procedure.
Erick: Here is a copy of my bitcoin wallet just click on the arrow in the right hand corner and it will walk you through what to do next, Ok?
Me: Yes, Erick I will let you know when the transaction is complete **Erick:** Ok, my love I will wait for you
Me: It shows the transaction is complete it says 30 minutes. Let me know you received the $1298 ok?
Erick: Yes, I saw a notification and I have confirmed it. Now I will forward your money for the Lithium investment to be activated. You have really impressed me honey. You deserve an accolade, my wife! Is there something that you've dreamed of doing for a long time?
Me: I have not been to a beach in 4 years and would love to visit.
Erick: Destiny has a place for you my love. Your time to be celebrated is now and I am excited for us my love and one of your values is optimism that is adorable and that's a trait I want by my side.
Me: I can handle anything as long as the end game is to be in your arms. Babe I need a date when you are coming to get me because my last day of work is May 10th and I figure that next week after I will need to finish up last minute ties here before I move in with you. And do things
Erick: Alright my precious I have no reason to allow you to stay there after your last day at work my love. So from now lets pray about it I will come the weekend of your last day at work so that we can have a week there to see everyone and do the things we have to do.
Me: Sounds good to me I pray everything stays on track.
Erick: Yes babe, we will keep doing what we are doing and

do not give in to any negativity because this is a big step for us both we have to remember always we made the choice and we are matured enough to make the right choices. I am in love with the woman you are and I know that my heart has found a home with you.

Me: I pray it all comes together

Erick: You are the type of woman who loves to be the brains behind the star and you derive joy to see what you are involved in to excel.

Me: You are probably correct with that assumption. I never craved the limelight but if someone else shines I have no problem in helping them attain their goals.

Erick: If you were able to live to age 90 and retain either the mind or body of a 30 year old for the last 60 years of your life, which would you choose?

Me: Definitely the mind because what is a young body without a strong mind. You can alter The body to look younger but you cannot regain what you lost as far as your mind.

Erick: You are a smart woman! I am proud of you.

I realized he constantly tested me with these strange questions to see how intelligent I was. Maybe it was to see where I best fit in his scheme of scamming. These scammers have many job titles, from participating in the direct scam to handling the finances to internet fraud with the victims' financial information and, of course, money laundering. Some women have been asked to go to another country and retrieve packages and take them to another country only to be caught and to find out they were trafficking drugs. This is a reality when dealing with these scammers. And most of us victims have no idea what we got ourselves into until it's too late. Most women are asked to set up bank accounts for them to launder money from or to send a bad check that eventually bounces for thousands of dollars, and then she is left with owing the bank what was lost. It's outrageous, because we, as victims, become victims of the system because these banks clear these checks only to have them bounce later.

Erick: Do you have a secret hunch about how you will die?

Me: No, that information is in God's hands not ours. Do you?

Erick: Yes, to have all my love ones beside me and have my family close and singing hymns with me to send me home.

Me: That is beautiful babe.

Erick: Name three things you and me as partners appear to have in common

Me: Patience, Humbled and Grace

Erick: You are indeed, my wife!

Me: Does that mean we match?

Erick: It means we are a perfect match, For what in your life do you feel most grateful?

Me: For life itself and the ability to love

Erick: You are a wise woman

Me: What are you most grateful for?

Erick: I am grateful for life, my family and you beautiful

Me: That is sweet babe **Erick:** Do you have knowledge of interior design?

Me: Yes, my love I love to decorate especially with a theme décor

Erick: I am thinking we can redecorate the house when you come

Me: That would be nice to decorate together, babe

Erick: How is your health? Are you looking after yourself now for me?

Me: Of course, my love! I am in good health right now. I just got to get through this move

Erick: I am glowing with pride because I have found what I'm looking for

Me: I am glad you are happy with pride I am excited for this next chapter in our life

Erick: I know you are a fruitful soul and any seed sown in you will give fruits so I consider myself a blessed man

Me: I am blessed because you are a beautiful soul and I am excited for the beautiful adventure we are embarking on babe

Erick: I am leaving to go home my love. I will be having dinner with some close associate
Me: That is good I am happy you are not eating alone, my love
Erick: hahaha my love it would be a happier feeling with you by my side
Me: Until then your associates will have to do
Erick: Hahaha, my sweet woman you are the best thing to happen to me this stage of my life. **Me:** I feel the same way about you too
Erick: We will talk more about Memorial Day
Me: I have a family function I need to attend that weekend and I do not want to miss it
Erick: We are a family now my love and how can we have a unique joint family memory. Do you think you are single?

At this point he was working overtime trying to control me and tried to tell me what I needed to do for us and the decisions I needed to make. He would bring up the "We are a family now and you are my wife" scenario a lot. Every day during our relationship it was "What are you doing?" "What are you eating?" "You need to take care of this and yourself for me." This is typical scammer rules: to control their clients and get them to believe that you are their partners and they needed to control you. I am thankful I am an independent person, but had I known this was how they worked, I would have been able to see the signs and stop this relationship. I had a lot of questions, but they would come later, and none of my questions were answered to my satisfaction.

Me: We can discuss this later, Ok?
Erick: I will also like you to meet the boys now they are even more curious to meet you
Me: I am excited to meet them also and I am sure they are curious about me, just as my family is curious to meet you.
Erick: You are my world now and I want you to be confident that I Erick Andersen have got and I will never let you down.

I want to welcome you home with a great ambience of love

Me: I will be honored to be by your side no matter what life throws at us we can handle it together and I will have nothing but love and devotion to our life together and whoever is attached to it

Erick: That is a realistic view and that also is one of the reasons I love you my queen because you always are not afraid to hit the nail on the head. I know sooner in a time not too far from now I will be coming back home to a sweet kiss and a sweet meal specially made by a queen for a king and we can also have a candle lit dinner my love with soft music

Me: You are the sweetest man on earth and I cannot wait to cook for you and of course kiss you. I am so excited for our new life together my heart is glowing with love.

Erick: That reminds me you asked about the lithium and the bitcoin but I forgot to respond

Me: Yes, last night when we were talking on the phone.

Erick: Yes, now I do my wife. I was saying that you have two advantages now to make an increase in bitcoin and you need to increase your investment fund spot to premium as this is the right time for premium investors who are potential shareholders in the company.

Me: Ok, so how does bitcoins go to lithium was my unanswered question?

Erick: You are so beautiful my love. Bitcoin is the platform accepted by the lithium producing company for investors to book their spot to invest and also receive dividends from their investment and to give the investor top class privacy and first hand control.

Me: Oh, that explains the connection and now I understand my husband. Next question is how long do you think the market will stay invigorated with bitcoins? Your personal opinion of course.

Erick: My love the main thing is that your bitcoin is the platform for you to invest and receive your dividend privately with no taxes, then on the other hand bitcoin has the advantage that you can sell and make more profit when it is high so imagine making a nice profit when you know how to trade it.

Again, I noticed that when I asked questions, he would delay in answering or not answer them at all. I guess I must have thrown him off his script, and he had to deter me from realizing he was not who he said he was. Remember, he portrayed himself as an investment specialist, so I would try to ask his opinion on investing, but he would sidestep me if he did not want to answer. I often wonder if I was talking to the same man at times because, keep in mind, these scammers work in groups and around the clock, because we are in different time zones, and his real time zone is five hours ahead of mine. One of the red flags was getting texts from him in the middle of the night, but Las Vegas is four hours behind my time zone, so I never really questioned that.

> **Me:** Ok, I understand now, babe
> **Erick:** I know you are smart and this is a good time my love and I really want you to increase your investment fund so that you have a huge advantage when you fully invest your fund and while we enjoy our life you will be growing financially.
> **Me:** I would love to invest in the future but I do not want to cut myself short on wrapping up residual ties here before I move.
> **Erick:** That is right my wise wife but how much can you push yourself now to invest further lets see what we can do?

Another incoming call, but we were cut off shortly afterward with the claim of bad reception. This is quite common with scammers to cut their phone conversations very short. I can actually say we never talked more than three or four minutes max during our relationship. I can actually say that most of the incoming calls were when he needed to push for more money for me to invest or if he thought I was mad at him.

> **Me:** I will try but I cannot make any promises, babe
> **Erick:** My love everyday our hope and faith in our creator is that we are getting closer to each other and our day to hold

each other is getting closer.

Me: Yes, it is Erick

Erick: I know that you are a daughter chosen by our creator to come and impact my generation just as much as I am destined to impact yours and this is why everyday brings us closer to each other and for our generations.

Me: You know I love you not only for your beautiful soul but for your awesome mind too, babe

Erick: You are a swift arrow in the hand of a mighty man and I know any target with you and any project with you is always going to be successful. We are going to enjoy this journey this is my promise to you my highness Queen Donna Andersen.

Me: I have no doubt we are going to have an awesome happy life together. Every day together is a blessing of love and devotion to one another that is what happens when you find your soulmate in life

Erick: I love you Donna Andersen! Thank you for coming to my world! Over and over I fall for you what would my life be without you in it? You complete me, baby. Your eyes, your smile, and everything about you is just perfect. You are the right one for me. What makes you feel the most alive.

Me: About you, your heart and soul does and your kindness and commitment and your love and faith, my love

Erick: That is great my love and I really love your answers because the only source to go through challenges and survive is things in faith in our creator and also genuine love and faith in you and by those around you. What replenishes your mind, body and spirit?

Me: Prayer and faith in god, babe

Erick: You've captured my mind, heart, body, soul and all. I do not want this feeling to end as it gives me thorough happiness

(Three more pictures were sent; one of just him standing next to a car and then of him with five other men and then the last of him socializing with two of the men in pictures.)

Me: Wow, you are so handsome babe
Erick: Thank you my love. I'm hosting some of the executive delegates for lunch and wine by the house my love. I know in a time not too far from now you will be by my side as a co-host too.
Me: I am looking forward to it, my love
Erick: I will continue to make you the best because I can see that there is so much love in your heart to share to a man that will love you.
Me: I love you, babe
Erick: This is the beginning my love and I gave you my promise that I have checked on your soul and you have a beautiful soul and you are full of life and openness and optimism only that you had met the wrong men in your life who did not see your potentials and were selfish not to open you to your full potential because they are afraid you will be more successful than them but I am a man that needs a woman with your potentials and when I found you it would be silly for me to let you go.
Me: That is very sweet that you feel that way about me. It makes me love you even more and you have a very sweet soul and I am counting on you to always feel this way. **Erick:** And you make me sleep great, my love
Me: You better get some rest now because you are going to need it because once we meet there will not be a whole lot of sleeping
Erick: Hahaha, I think I can't wait for that one, my love. You are a amazing soul and I am blessed to be your man
Me: Yes, you are definitely blessed, babe Another picture of him and four men walking along a street was sent to me
Erick: I'm proud of the impact I have made in the lives of these men, my love

Me: I am proud of you as a good business man, you are my hero for what you have accomplished and I love you too!

Erick: Yes, my love integrity is everything. That is your best currency is your integrity and thank you my love and you are my mighty arrow. I know that you are the woman chosen by destiny even as a reward from our creator and also I am sure my late wife approved of you also.

Me: That is very sweet babe, I love you

Erick: We have not concluded what we are going to do for Memorial Day. You do realize that we are going to be living together by then.

Me: I know we are going to be combining our lives together, that is why I am working so hard dismantling my life here. What do you want to do for Memorial Day? I am easy to please Are the boys coming for the Holiday?

Erick: Yes, they should my love I believe we will conclude before then Ok?

Me: Sounds good to me

Erick: Is that alright with you that the boys will spend the holiday with us?

Me: Of course, babe they are part of the package

Erick: Honey, I want our beginning to begin in a memorable way for you and me and also for our kids because our lives have begun together a new book has been opened for us by destiny it is in our hands now to write each chapter with a golden pen and I know that each line will be of beautiful memories together.

Me: I have no doubts we will have a memorable life together. God has put us in place to meet in this lifetime together for this next chapter in our lives. We can work together to overcome any challenges that come our way and your boys are a part of our new life too.

Erick: That is what makes us one big happy family in our kingdom where I am the king and you my queen. I have prayed my entire life for God to deliver to me a woman as

caring, as forthright and as passionate as you. We are truly ordained to be together under heaven for all time.
Me: I love you, my king
Erick: My mom said she was visited by her prayer group and there was a prophecy for us!
Me: What prophecy for us, my love?
Erick: That there is going to be a celebration soon
Me: Of course, babe
Erick: I want to be the friend you fall hopelessly in love with. The one you take into your arms And into your bed and into your private world you keep trapped in your head. I want to be that kind of friend the one the one who will memorize the things you say as well as the shape of your lips when you tell them. I want to know every curve, every freckle, every shiver of your body. I want to know where to touch you, I want to know how to convince you to design a smile just for me. Yes, I do want to be your friend. I want to be your best friend in the entire world. If my love were an ocean, there would be no more land. If my love were a desert, you would see only sand. If my love were a starlit night only light. And if my love could grow wings, I'd be soaring in flight.
Me: I love you my beautiful soulmate
Erick: I love you Donna Andersen, You are my sun and sky where night will never set. I will always see your bright joy, burning in my heart, loving me, casting my grace on you, and with that joy and love I will build a cathedral of our lives that we will live in splendor and joy.
Me: And this is why I will always place my love and faith in you, Mr. Andersen
Erick: I do really means, I will. I will dedicate myself to you. I will take your hand in a spirit of adventure. I will respect your decisions even when I might not agree with them. I will stand by you. I will love you and love growing old with you.
Me: I am a very easy person to live with because it is my nature. I will respect your decisions because I know in my soul

you will have our best interest in mind. I doubt I will ever need to question your motives or beliefs because they are the same as mine. You are a brilliant man and I admire that about you.

Erick: I love your laugh, I love your spirit, I love that I will spend the rest of my life with you. I love the thought of growing old with you and fighting through challenges, embracing joy, from this moment till the end of time.

Me: I feel the same about you. Do you know most people will walk this earth and never meet their soulmate? I feel so cherished to have this once in a lifetime opportunity to have you in my life, I know every day will be filled with love and devotion to one another. My heart is so filled with happiness because of you entering my life.

Erick: Every new day I look forward to each day with the joy of knowing that my tomorrow includes you. And I feel blessed that you accepted to be my best friend and my wife and to stand hand in hand, side by side and heart to heart together to into love our destiny has seeded in our hearts for each other.

(He sent me a Lithium Market Stock price update to keep me knowing I invested wisely.)

Erick: I love you my wife, you see lithium is on the high. I am hoping it will still be up until you are ready to fully fund your investment.
Me: I am keeping my fingers crossed that can happen, babe
Erick: I know you are but any news with your retirement funds my wife
Me: I will not receive any retirement until June so I will have to make due until then
Erick: That is cool my wife. Because a long journey for us is ahead. Honey do you like to speak in public?
Me: Only if I have too! I am a introvert I am more comfort-

Scammed in America

able in smaller groups versus large groups.
Erick: Did I tell you I am building an investment academy?
Me: Like a training academy for investing?
Erick: Yes, my love

(He sent me three pictures of looking like from a seminar. He also sent six photos of a series of cars some with his late wife Anita in them.)

Erick: Would you want something different than one of these cars?
Me: It does not matter as long as I can touch the pedal you know I have short legs, babe
Erick: Hahaha, you are a very sweet girl. You know my favorite is the Bentley and that is the one I intend to come with my love if that is alright with you? I want to make you very comfortable.
Me: Whatever your comfortable with is fine by me
Erick: Alright my love, are you ready my love?
Me: Ready to move?
Erick: Yes, with me! Are you getting nervous?
Me: I am very excited but not nervous, babe
Erick: I love you my beautiful woman you always speak the words I expect from my partner!
Me: I am going to book us a suite at a hotel for when you come so we can be comfortable Until we are ready to leave. Any suggestions or preferences in hotels?
Erick: Whatever you choose is alright my queen. I want you to understand that I am a man that enjoys quality times with my family now that you are coming into my world I believe you are prepared for the new book opened for us by our creator and I believe in you that we will write each chapter with the golden pen of love and happiness, peace understanding, oneness and honesty because now it is in our hands to decide how our readers will be inspired when they read our book of the impact we made while we lived and shared with them

from our children and close friends and the world around us to bring praises to our creator for sending us to live among them or whoever we may come in contact with them while we live. This is my belief and prayer that my soulmate will also catch the same vision with me and together we enjoy the journey of writing our book as Mr. & Mrs. Andersen. I hope you know what I mean, honey

Me: I know exactly what you mean and I am so excited for this next chapter as one and I am over the moon with excitement for this union with you.

Erick: Honey have you ever been to award dinner?

Me: I have been to seminars but not award dinners, babe

Erick: This was the last one I shared with my partner

A series of photos with was his supposed-to-be late wife Anita was sent along with forty-seven other photos! These consisted of different family photos mostly of him with his late wife and two boys. They were of different scenarios from dinners, shopping, traveling, and adventures. Then a series of twenty more photos came across. I was at work, and my phone was pinging like crazy. I did not understand the significance of the number of photos sent all at once. A little overselling himself is the only conclusion I can come to. At this point I have literally thousands of photos sent, and some were duplicates of his family that were stolen from another person's Facebook or Instagram page. For some of us victims, we don't look at the other victims in the scam because they have not given thousands of dollars or are in financial ruin, but they are victims, because if they are successful at attaining large amounts of money and they use this person's photos over and over with other victims, and it becomes never-ending for them. In most cases, the other victim is blamed for the scam. This is true because the other victim I know of from Erick truly believes the man in the photos is the scammer and his family and associates are involved. I have done investigation myself, and I found that this is not true. I have watched videos over and over of the real man in the photos and his voice does have an accent but does not match the man I talked to with for a year. The man in the photos is American and has an education and his mannerisms did not match. There were a lot of inconsistencies in the timeline and stories that were fed to me. For example, Erick started conversing with me in March 2019, and the man in the photos was on a family vacation during this time, and we were in constant contact throughout this time period. There is no way this man in the photos could have spent his vacation with his family constantly texting and video chatting with me at the same time.

> **Me:** That was a lot of photos especially of your past. I have to question whether you are ready to move forward and leave the past behind you!
>
> **Erick:** Well I only concluded that she was needed for a more assignment in heaven and that the woman destined to end the rest of my year will come my way hence I was able to heal and now very optimistic though it was not easy. I also tried to be in a relationship 3 years after she passed away but the lady almost ruined me but what does not kill you only makes you stronger and now here I am in a new chapter with you my love and isn't it amazing, no wonder they say the end is always better than the beginning.
>
> **Me:** I am sorry but you need understand I need you to be on the same page not compare me to a past relationship. I love you and I am willing to start this new chapter with you but I need a promise that the past will stay in the past. That is needed in order to have a clean slate for the future. I am asking for your patience and I will grant you the same in return, my love.
>
> **Erick:** You know it's never easy to heal and I will be glad to heal your heart with the love you deserve.
>
> **Me:** I know love heals all wounds, babe
>
> **Erick:** Do you know the saying that iron sharpens iron? That is how you and I will grow and everyday I am getting excited about the triumphant entry and coming of my Queen and I pray always for guidance and a sweet creative way to welcome you in a way you will never forget.
>
> **Me:** We will be together within the next week this is the hardest part out with the old life and in with the new life. I am

so excited but so exhausted too.

Erick: Thank you my love and I want to also tell you I am a very creative man from singing to playing musical instruments, I also did graphic designs and I collect art which you will also see when you come home my wife and I write as well. My prayer was to find a woman that is also artistic for instance Mark has already started his own clothing line and Logan is a good artist as well. My late wife was a creative interior decorator and now God has blessed me with a pure woman in you that bears a womb of creativity and now you have to begin to tell me where your passion lies as well because I am here to lead you to live to your full potential as my wife and your patience should be fueled by the fact that you and I are going to be stronger by the fruits that will bear forth from this very phase that we are facing right now mentally, physically, spiritually, financially and environmentally. fear is going to be around you but it is in your power to rebuke and resist and then the fear will flee.

Me: It is obvious that I placed my faith and love into this relationship, but you understand that I am sacrificing for it. You understand that I walked away from a bad marriage and I rebuilt my life. As far as decisions I have a lot on my plate right now and don't want to bite off more than I can chew.

Erick: My dear sweetheart, I want to make a confession today. You know before I met you, I used to laugh at people who fell in love through internet dating and I used to make fun of them. I did not believe in the concept of love through internet dating but today I have the chance to tell you have completely changed my notion in life. Since the time you entered my life, I started loving you more and I love myself for falling in love with you. What is this and how has this happened I don't know. But I have found my true soulmate in you. Today, I believe that if love exists it's only because of you.

Me: I feel the same way, that is why I am sacrificing everything for a new life with you. I hope all of our dreams come true and we are able to put the past behind us and start anew as we close in on our new life as one, my love.

Erick: Love has no definition in life. When you love someone you feel it from your heart. you don't know what it feels like, but you never ever want to part. I am so glad I met you and we are starting a new life together. It is pure love and that is only true baby! You are the only reason in my life! And I will keep telling you everyday as long as I live to say that I love you Donna Andersen.

Me: That is beautiful Babe! You are a real sweetheart how did I get so lucky? I love you, Mr. Erick Andersen

Erick: You are safe with me now I will look after you and you can be rest assured that I will never let you down, my love.

Me: What are you doing, babe?

Erick: I am writing an article on an enterprising guidelines for a free resources by a non profit organization in my country of youths.

Me: I love that you help the less fortunate especially the youth.

Erick: Thank you, my love. You are also my motivation to help others. You are the best thing that I never saw ahead of me, baby. You are that woman who will transform my imperfections into perfections, just by the touch of your love. You are the woman that will hold my hand and together we will pray together, laugh with me, celebrate with me and I will also transform your imperfections to perfection and you weaknesses to strength and your fears to faith, your sorrow to laughter and your pain to joy and I will also make you admire and cherish yourself daily because when you are at your best then definitely I get the best from you.

Me: Awww, I love you my beautiful soulmate you are a sweetheart.

Erick: Did you hear about the bombing in Sri Lanka?

Me: Yes, it happened Easter what a horrible tragedy and so little disregard for human life. I do not understand how

> someone can take another life because of their religious or for political purpose.
> **Erick:** It is really sad to see the level of sorrow religious fanaticism is causing humanity
> **Me:** The sad part is these terrorist groups train their children that this hatred is OK.
> **Erick:** So I am looking into reaching out to the families of the affected victims honey.

I noticed throughout our relationship he would make mention of watching CNN and keeping up on current affairs around the world. It also seemed, especially the in the last couple of phone calls, like I could hear what seemed to be a television on but could not make out what channel or if it was news or movies. He has actually sent me pictures of his computer screen and computer desk, so I know he worked in a room separate from others, either a hotel room or an apartment. As I am going over all the text messages, I am seeking whether he worked alone or with others. Most scammers work with others, as one will pick up the storyline as the other scammer leaves off. That is another reason they keep notes on all of their victims, or clients, as they refer to us as. He would also repeat things I told him months earlier, and some things he had said months earlier he would also repeat. I am assuming he had a new client and was baiting her too with the same lines. He seemed to stick with the script he had laid out because if I asked questions, he would not answer immediately, so he was not freestyling his scam.

> **Me:** That would be a good thing to do, you are such a resourceful man, Erick
> **Erick:** Yes, as ambassadors of the kingdom of heaven of love, peace and forgiveness we have to practice what we preach by reaching out to those relatives of those affected. My love, I am excited and delighted to have your precious presence and begin to take your place as the mother of the Andersen's and the Queen of Erick!
> **Me:** I am excited too! I cannot wait, babe
> **Erick:** Thank you my love. Words from my soul that cannot

be contained, feelings that I have wanted so much to share with you today this evening. I just returned home from watching a movie by myself and realizing I left so much unsaid this afternoon. Remembering that I could still write to you like this, even if you would not see it right away. I drove around for fifteen minutes just listening to the songs you sent me from your favorite songs and listening to your voice. This is the first time I have woken up everyday in over three years super excited about the future with someone I can call my woman confidently and boldly. A little traveling music was what I needed and I wanted to write this letter to you and let you know that you and I are forever, you know that? I want to spend the rest of my life with you and I know you feel the same. Together we will decide the best way to do that.

We sent YouTube videos of our favorite music to one another. I sent him videos of my favorite music songs. and he did the same. Most of mine was blues, rock, and R&B, where he sent me mostly R&B or pop love songs.

Erick: You make me fly but in a safe way I have never known before. Because of you I am not afraid to be me, to be the person I was always meant to be. You could not have given me a greater gift than if you took all your money and spent it all on me. The greatest gifts I have found in you and these words are from my heart. You have all my love and you always have since the day we met. I find there is no life without you in it to share it with. Nothing is too hard, nothing is impossible because of you. You make me believe that anything is possible. I am sitting here on the stairs but my thoughts are miles away to wherever you are this evening. Wishing so much I could touch your face, your hair and see that beautiful smile. Just to run my fingers down the side of your face would be heaven to me. Just to look in your eyes and see what I have been waiting to see. Just to let you look in to my eyes and see my soul as I know you have been waiting to do. The truth of my feelings for you is more than mere words could express. I love you is not enough for what you do to me not do I doubt your motives anymore but you didn't know that did you. I was not sure for a long time that I will ever feel this way about a woman even after I was hurt by the other lady I had in my life that I have cared about. I do not know if my messages was clear but I just feel overwhelmed by the way you make me feel. I would rather spend one lifetime with you than face all the ages of the world alone. I love you my dear Donna Andersen.

It was not unusual for me to get very long messages from him, especially love letters. It came across after a long day of not hearing anything but normal "I love you" messages from him. I now know he had two or more other women he was wooing, so he would have to eventually return to me to keep me on the hook because time was getting closer to when we were supposed to be together. The second weekend of May 2019 was the date set for us to be together, and we were within a week away.

Me: Thank you for the beautiful letter I really needed it I am exhausted from packing and still working and really needed a pick me up. I hope you know how much I am looking forward to our first meeting and for the rest of my life to spend with you, babe.
Erick: I do not know the official definition of WIFE but for me it means the Woman who is Independent and Fun loving and Eternally in love with me. You fit that definition perfectly. I love you, baby
Me: You fit the definition of the perfect husband to be for me. A loving soulmate with a beautiful heart who is kind and considerate. Oh and you have nice legs too. That is always a bonus!
Erick: Thank you my love and your mother-in-law sends her regards. Did I tell you I am considering going back to school?
Me: Did you tell her I am excited to meet her? You know I

will support any endeavor you choose. What are you considering taking classes for, my love

Erick: I know in some days from now you will the first face and person I see when you wake up in the morning and the last face I see before I go to bed and I agree that you become like half of the person you spend most of your time with and that comes with the wisdom of the law of attraction so I am always carefully and patiently choosing those I attract into my world not to talk about the woman I am going to spend the rest of my living with and so you can be assured that my search has lead me to you and I want to know everything about you so that I can understand the woman that you are and how I can bring out the best of you because when you are your best it means definitely the man behind you will benefit just as much as when a great woman is behind a man. He is always successful that is why people can recognize and say behind every successful man is a successful woman and because I have found her before and I know the joy it brings before heavens called her for a greater duty while positioning my path to find the woman that will complete the rest of my life with me, I hope you understand that I am glad I have found you now and I have to nurture you to be the best for us.

Me: I hope you understand that it will take us some time to get in synchronicity with one another we come from different backgrounds and counties but with love and patience anything is possible. That being said I cannot wait to fall asleep in your arms and awake to your beautiful face every morning. I fell in love with you as a person not what you can or cannot provide and I know together we can survive anything coming our way. I know we will always improve one another but it will be the love for one another that will see us through.

Erick: Thank you for having so much faith in me and in us as a couple. Thank you for making me a better person, for

giving me your heart and for letting me give you mine. Our relationship has developed into something wonderful. I can't imagine spending time with anyone else now or having such deep feelings for anyone else either. I am truly honored to be yours and I love you.
Me: That is beautiful Mr. Andersen and I love you too for your beautiful heart and soul and and I cannot wait to see your beautiful face in a week!
Erick: What are you doing my love
Me: Going through paperwork babe
Erick: Alright my love did you buy the outfit you wanted to buy?
Me: No, I have not bought anything especially clothes! I am looking to get rid of most of my clothes not accumulate any more.
Erick: You know you should not buy much
Me: I have not bought anything except for food in over a month, babe

I was very confused over this conversation as to where the question of me buying an outfit came from, because he insisted I was shopping. I now realize he was confusing me with another victim who may have mentioned shopping for an outfit. If he was constantly going back and forth between us, it would only make sense that he would get us mixed up in conversation. Hence comes the notetaking he has mentioned making throughout our relationship. But, like all humans, he has made errors, and I think I just overlooked those signs that things were not what they appeared to be.

Erick: I should be going back to Miami in the next couple days, my love
Me: Miami? Do you mean Vegas, my love
Erick: Vegas baby! I will be leaving Miami to Vegas is what I meant to say. My most priority now is to round up from here and back to Vegas so I can begin to prepare for us to be together. I do not want to be in a hurry when we are together

that is why I want to finish up with my presentations here my love.

Me: I know you are working hard too and I appreciate you everyday and I am getting excited for your arrival and cannot wait to see you.

Erick: Thank you for understanding, my wife I was finding and seeking and now that I have found you I am not searching anymore I just want to enjoy every day in the knowledge of you until we are together to begin to enjoy the knowledge we have about each other in trust ambience we know we have found a home for our hearts in our worlds.

Me: You are a sweetheart and I cannot wait to wrap my arms around your neck and kiss you

Erick: My love, I need your email address

Me: Ok, just send me yours and I will reply then you will have mine OK?

Erick: Iamerickandersen500@gmail.com is my email my wife

Me: Did you receive my email with my address yet?

Erick: Yes, I love you baby and you will receive your certificate from my admin department because it has been received from the lithium association

Me: Will I need to print it?

Erick: Yes, laminate and keep it safe, my wife. This is a standard investor certificate and I want you to get the premium. Should we have it on hold and extend to you or do you want this copy mailed to you, my love?

Me: Just have them mail it to your address, I am going to be there in a week or so, babe

Erick: My love you are most amazing

Me: I already directed all my mail to your address in Las Vegas you gave me

Erick: Alright my wife, I am hopelessly in love with you and I want to be that special someone with whom you are hopelessly in love with. I want to be the best friend for you and the kind of friend whom you could hug tight in your arms,

the one you would like to cuddle within our bed. I want you to let me in your private world that is only yours. Show me the deepest and most secret thoughts which you keep trapped in your head. I promise to be the kind of friend who will cherish the memories of all things you say and the shape of your lips when you tell them. I am eager to discover every inch of your body, every curve and every freckle. I want to know where to touch you and how to touch you. I want to see your smile that is designed just for me. Yes, I do want to be that kind of friend, the best one in the entire world.
Me: That is beautiful babe! I cannot wait to see your handsome face and have you hold me in your arms. I promise to give you my heart and soul for you to keep in a safe place and I cannot wait for the endless days of laying in your arms and listening to you talk about your days and confide in me your fears and dreams. I love you and will cherish every minute of our time together, I cannot wait to be Mrs. Andersen!
Erick: Thanks to the stars above, we came together. At first it was just a liking, but soon enough it turned into deep love. I won't lie, I felt something in my heart when I first saw your profile on Zoosk. That something was certain, something that told me that the feeling I got was true. And know I know that I have been waiting for since my late wife passed away and now I will feel the power of love and this this power I have found in love with you.

I did receive a certificate of lithium purchase via text. I now know it was fake; they produce fake documents to everything, passports, identifications, airline tickets, letters, etc. Later, I received a notice from USPS that the address he provided for my mail did not exist! As you will see in the following texts, he has a answer and excuse for every issue that arises.

Me: Love, I just got a notification from the Post Office not recognizing your address in their system as a valid address?
Erick: Really my love! If our house in Vegas I will share our

location with you when I get home Because sometimes the address kicks up the children park, my love

Me: What is your email address that way you can see the email the USPS sent me regarding the existence of your Vegas address.

Erick: Iamerickandersen500@gmail.com

Me: That way you can print it off and take it into Post Office in Vegas and straighten it out when you get back home before you come get me, babe

Erick: No words can possibly express the vow that I give you now – it is a part of myself that I place in your care as we join together.

Me: Always remember home is wherever I am with you. No matter where life's journey takes us, we always have one another to fall back on. I am always available for you 24/7, no matter what mountain we climb, no matter what ocean we cross my home is always wherever you are, Mr. Erick Andersen.

(He sent a selfie of him behind the wheel of a car with sunglasses on.)

Me: Love that sweet face of yours

Erick: Thank you my love! How many more days left my baby!

Me: less than a week babe so excited to see you soon

Erick: I am sorry you will be under my watch soon, my love. I am looking forward with excitement too! I should be done here tomorrow so I can leave Saturday or Sunday my love. I want to go get ready for your arrival. Honey, my flight leaves at 11:45 P.M. for Vegas

I received two pictures, one of which was an actress with a beautiful red dress with birds on it, and the other was of colorful men's shirts, island style, but I now know are typical Nigerian clothing. They are pullover tunic styles only found in Africa. There was no comment made by either, but I think it was a test to see if I would notice. He made mention in conversations he would like to see me in red. Even though the man in the all of the pictures dressed well, I had not seen any of the attire in the pictures on him. I later received video of him on a plane, not speaking. The video lasted two seconds and was time stamped for 11:46 P.M. to coincide with the time he said he was flying home.

> **Erick:** How can you tell the day not to be bright when its morning, how can you tell the trees not to dance when the wind blows, how can you tell the rain not to fall when the clouds are gloomy, how can you tell me not to love when you exist, its impossible my dear queen Donna Andersen you have nurtured my heart with your lovely heart of gold and I give praises to heaven that you were formed specifically for me to complete the remaining years of my life from glory to glory.
> **Me:** I love you, my Erick Andersen! I give you my heart, my promise, that I will walk with you, hand in hand, wherever our journey leads us, living, learning, loving, together, forever!
> **Erick:** I want to give you everything in my world to make you happy and fulfilled everyday you live with me. My wife they are coming to take the car for service today so I can make sure we are safe for travel.
> **Me:** Good, my love
> **Erick:** My wife I have updated my PA that you are upgrading your investment and the lithium management so that your award will be ready for me to present to you personally and also to make it to Japan together. We are going to shop for our matching outfit together, OK?
> **Me:** Yes, my love I cannot wait to shop with you and of course eventually upgrading my investment.
> **Erick:** This year the award ceremony will be black carpet event
> **Me:** Black Carpet? What is that?
> **Erick:** Is like red carpet but black carpet is more elegant for

elegant class
Me: Wow, it sounds nice. When is it love?
Erick: Around August, my love
Me: Wow, that is only 3 months away, babe.
Erick: They say the person that loves wins life, I am glad I have won with the best partner by my side, I know you are the reason I exist, I am made for you, I am really happy I have you in my life.
Me: I feel so blessed to have you in my life, every day I thank god for blessing me in this lifetime with a beautiful soulmate I have in you.

I received an incoming phone call with him it lasted 2:41 minutes. Most of our phone calls consisted of him talking, asking how I was doing and telling me he loved and missed me. Sometimes he said he was preparing for a meeting or had a project he was working on. Never any details of work or where he was at other than at home or ready to leave to office. I understand they keep their phone calls short for the reason of not being traceable, and every single phone they use is untraceable too. This is standard protocol for scammers.

Erick: I bless the day I met you because being your friend has really changed my life, falling in love with you was beyond my control, you are one in a million, you are priceless, you are very precious to me and I will love you forever.
Me: You are a very precious man to me too, babe What are you doing my love? Did you go to post office and take care of your address issues?
Erick: I am leaving to the Bahamas today to go get our boys, honey!
Me: How long are you going to be there?
Erick: I should leave there tomorrow, my love
Me: I miss you and be safe
Erick: I am excited, my wife It is clear to me now that everything in my life has led me to you. I think back on all my choices and consider even the bad ones blessed because if I

had done even one thing differently, I might never have met you and become your husband.
Me: God steered both of our paths to this time in our lives. I now know everything has happened for a reason for us to be together.
Erick: I need your blockchain wallet ID, honey
Me: I don't have a blockchain account but a Coinbase account. I will send you that ID, OK?
Erick: I received a dividend on your lithium for $15.15 for you today and I am sending it to your wallet.
Me: Ok, I will let you know when the transaction is confirmed, babe

He sent me a snapshot of the notification, but I think it was intended to lure me to invest more money. Up until then, I only gave the initial thousand dollars for investing. But in order to sell me the story on me investing in lithium stock, he had to up his game and give me a dividend on my investment to continue this relationship.

Erick: Let me know as soon as you receive an alert, my wife
Me: I received the payment into my account, my love please text me when you land, OK?
Erick: We have landed back in Vegas now. The love I give you is very true it will never go sour even in the most difficult times, my love will grow stronger daily because you are my source of joy and I simply cannot do this relationship thing without you, my love.
Me: I am so happy you and the boys are home safe. I am the happiest woman on earth because of your love and devotion to us. I cannot wait to see your beautiful smile and wrap my arms around your handsome neck
Erick: I have no doubt about your love for me, my love I am waiting for the delivery of my car today
Me: When are they delivering it?
Erick: I was told today, babe

Me: Wow, then I won't see you till Sunday then if you drive because today is Thursday and it takes 48 hours to drive here from there, babe

Erick: My love, really? Let me think, my love

Erick: My love

Me: What is the plan? Babe I have people coming from out of town to meet you here and you will not be here! I told everyone you would be here tomorrow, you understand what I am saying?

Erick: My love can they wait till Sunday morning?

Me: No, this was arranged in advance and some have to work Sunday

Erick: Will they need me to bring any gift of apology?

Me: They will be sorely disappointed and I really needed you to help me with the move too!

Erick: My wife, I will treat you right and give you things that money cannot buy, morning and night and noon I will cling to you and would not say goodbye, When you need myself I will be there for you standby, my love will never die!

Me: All I ask for is for you to communicate with me and with honesty. I cannot say I am not extremely disappointed you will not be here tomorrow but I know you had a lot to deal within the past week and I know something are out of your control right now. Just let me know when you leave and communicate when you can.

Erick: I love you my darling honey

Me: Are you on your way?

Erick: Please I will communicate with you shortly, my precious woman

It was a trying day. I cleaned out my apartment except with what I was taking, and of course, my cats were still there at the apartment. I had paid for the whole month of May so I had to clean and turn in the keys prior to my departure, so I felt the cats would be more comfortable there then in a hotel. It was a bittersweet day because I had to rebuild my life after my divorce, so everything I gave up that day I worked really hard to have. I had a two-bedroom apartment packed full of furnishings and a lot of clothes. I sold a lot, but I donated and gave away to family members too. I was exhausted. It has only been seven months since my back surgery, and lifting still really hurt.

> **Erick:** God has given me a woman that has proven to be a beautiful mother, a wonderful wife, And an amazing friend. I am thankful to God for you being such a blessing in my life and To our generation. Your friendship, your commitment to our family, and your love define My life. Life is wonderful because of you! Happy Mothers Day!
> **Me:** I need you babe! When are you coming?

I came back to the apartment and found out one of my cats was missing. It seemed my nephew grabbed a bag with my comforter, and one of the cats was hiding in it, so she spent the night in his truck. I had to go meet my sister to retrieve it. I did not hear back from Erick till the next morning, so I was staying in a hotel for two days waiting for his arrival and checking on the cats and cleaning the apartment to stay busy.

> **Erick:** I will treat you right and give you things money cannot buy morning, night and noon. I will cling to you and won't say goodbye. When you need me I will be there for you my love will reign forever and will never die!
> **Me:** My love, are you arriving today? Why have I not heard for you? I tried calling in case you were driving?
> **Erick:** My queen, When the day comes when your hair is grey, I hope you understand deep in your heart that my love will still be strong and I will always be true. I have to say this was the first time during this relationship that I had felt that maybe I jumped in too soon.

In a span of two days, I dismantled my life and had no idea if this was going to work. I felt doubt seep into my decision to be with him. He was supposed to be here initially Saturday morning, then moved to Sunday morning;

now, by Sunday night, no excuse or answers, and I was feeling like I may have made a mistake in trusting him. I booked a hotel for four days and paid in full; then what if he didn't show? I had an empty apartment for two weeks; then I was essentially homeless! Later that evening, I received a text with explanation.

Erick: Where are you?
Me: At the hotel waiting on you, babe
Erick: Alright my love. My mom fell sick and was rushed to the hospital that's where I have been they said it was food poisoning. I know you will be disappointed. I wrote a prayer today that I wanted to share with you.
Me: Why am I just hearing about this? That is terrible you just came from Bahamas and now you had to fly back. I was worried something happened to you on the road, babe. Please give her my love and keep me informed.
Erick: Did you get her the angel, my love?
Me: The angel is safe I cleaned it and shrink wrapped it for transport to her. What is the prayer you wrote?
Erick: Lord make me an instrument of your peace. Where there is hatred let me show love. Where there is injury Pardon. Where there is doubt Faith. Where there is despair Hope. Where there is darkness Light. And where there is sadness Joy. Whether there is giving that we receive it is in pardoning that we are pardoned and it is in dying that we are born into eternal life, Amen
Me: Erick, that is beautiful and I cannot wait to pray with you!
Erick: I love you
Me: I love you too! And keep me informed of my future mother in law
Erick: Yes, I will my love. What are you doing?
Me: Relaxing I am exhausted from the move. Are the boys with you?
Erick: No, my love I left them because it was an emergency
Me: You are a wonderful father and I cannot wait to meet

them, my love

Erick: I am madly in love with a girl. I cannot stay without talking to her. I really cannot stay without looking at her. She even comes in my dreams. Day by day my love for her is increasing. I know I truly love and I want to be with her. She is the reason why I feel so good. You know who that girl is? It is you honey I simply love you!

Me: You are a beautiful talented poet, my love. For a beautiful gift to me you should write these in a book for me in your own handwriting. I love you my soulmate!

Erick: How are you doing, my wife?

Me: Missing you babe. How is my mother in law?

Erick: She is still in coma my love but responding to treatment

Me: Erick, how are you doing? I am praying for her and if she is responding to treatment that means she is fighting. She is a strong woman.

Erick: That's right, I love you! I was afraid I lost you and I don't know what I did to deserve such love

Me: You deserve all the love in the world and I know your mother would agree also.

Erick: I consider myself the most blessed man alive. How is your Coinbase and you should be getting some dividends from bitcoin and this week also from lithium.

Me: It is gaining but I did not know if the trade war with China would affect it because it affected the stock market.

Erick: This one is digital and how much has it gained so far?

Me: Four dollars so far, babe

Erick: Really it should be growing when you transact more.

Me: Yes, but I am hoping to invest more soon at this point I do not want to deplete my finances until you arrive. I need money to live off of for now.

Erick: You are a team player my co-captain

Me: Yes, and thank you for believing in us babe!

Erick: Thank you for stealing my eyes from the crowd and

stealing my heart from me. I love you and I will always love you forever and ever. You have sweetened and warmed up my life.
Me: You warm my heart, Mr. Andersen
Erick: My love I sent for the boys and I am waiting for their arrival here. I am hoping she gains consciousness so that I can come to you.
Me: I have faith she will it is that at her age it takes longer from them to recover from a trauma. I am glad the boys are coming they will be a comfort to you during this trying time.
Erick: I love you my wife and I will not let you down!

At this point I do not know what exactly was going on, but I only booked the hotel for four days, so I decided to check out and go stay with my brother till Erick arrived. It had been one week since I moved but still had the empty apartment for another twelve days. I do not know where my mail was and where it was going. I actually went to the post pffice to see if it was there, but they said they returned it to sender! I had very important paperwork coming, and now I had to try and track it down. Eventually I just changed my change-of-address to my brother's, but it took months to retrieve past mail.

Me: I love you too!
Erick: Are you missing work? I'm going to make you busy soon and you will only rest in my bed.
Me: I am not missing work and I am staying busy wrapping up loose ties here and waiting to hear from you, my husband.
Erick: You should be getting your seeking dividend this week.
Me: I am more excited for your arrival than a dividend. You are more important right now.
Erick: My wife I love you and Mom was taken to another ward.
Me: Is everything ok?
Erick: Yeah, I am hoping she needs a surgery from a specialist
Me: What kind of surgery, my love?

Erick: For pains in her waist

Me: Intestinal surgery?

Erick: Her waist needs some fluid that is wear all of her severe pains she is suffering from

Me: When are they doing the surgery?

Erick: I have contacted one of my specialist doctor friend from Brazil

Me: Is she strong enough for surgery or are you waiting to see what the specialist says?

Erick: I am sorry love. This is also affecting you too.

Me: I am very worried about her and her health and I wish I was there to comfort you during this trying time. Love and support is all I can offer from afar.

Erick: You make me really emotional. And I promise to you that I will never let you down.

Me: How is my future husband and mother-in-law?

Erick: My love I had to hire the services of a specialist because I don't like the pace of the previous Doctor and my family doctor is on vacation and is unreachable because he is at sea.

Me: That is a wise choice! Sometimes you need a different set of eyes to see clearer. I suggest you always go with your gut instinct especially in critical medical care. I pray for you and your family at this time.

Erick: Firstly, they transferred her late to another ward that I wasn't happy about then secondly I was not impressed with the way the doctor went about handling my mom. He did not seem to realize she's in an emergency and wanted to go through unnecessary long protocols which I'm even willing and offered to pay for to boycott.

Me: It seems unfortunate you have to police her healthcare but not all doctors have what is in the best interest of the patient in mind. I am glad you are there for her and I think she will benefit from a specialist point of view.

Erick: I never knew I could love this much. A love so pure and true. Flowing endlessly as the waters of the ocean. Going all the way like eternity was on earth. My love for you will do no wrong. It wouldn't hurt even if I hurt. Your happiness will be my goal every night and day. I'll say to my heart all day long, it has done well to love you. My offering of love will always be at your table awaiting the blessings of your heart. I can't wait to have you close to me. It's you or nobody else, my love

Me: You are the most beautiful heart I have ever met in a man. You are always on my mind and my heart breaks you are going through this but remember you are not alone. I am always with you in your heart and soul and that love is stronger than most love. I will always be here for you, my Erick.

I received a second message; it was a copy of the last message, then he immediately deleted it saying, "My message delivered twice my love." I now know there was another woman he was corresponding with at the same time, and I think he was sending her the same messages simultaneously. It would be revealed later, but he also met her on Zoosk dating app. The repeating of the same quotes and messages to me seemed to be more frequent as our relationship moved on.

Erick: You are an amazing woman and all I can say Mrs. Dorothy Andersen come have your way in my heart, come take your place in my home. No matter how tough it gets, this road will lead me to only one heart. That heart is where I hope to lay my pillow and have a Very sound sleep at night. It is where I imagine my thoughts will linger every day and night, I say to you, my love, I crave for your warmth more than life itself.

Me: I know our life together will be the most precious time in our lives. I have total faith in you my love, because I trust you with the most precious thing my heart and soul.

Erick: Be the light of my world, be my friend indeed. Be the wife I dream of even when my eyes are opened. Be the mother of my kids and the one I find by my side every time of the night. I hope you be my all in all because that is what I want to be for you. I hope you would let me be your man, now and in the days to come. Let me be your man, now and in the days to come. Let me be the best of your love in the best way there is. Let me be the shoulder you lean on in times of need. Let me be all that you ever dream of because I'll let you be the woman you are for me and together we will be hand in hand enjoying the joy of old age in love and I hope you know what I mean my love.

Me: I love you my Erick Andersen and I will never tire of telling you this everyday

Erick: I love you, my love

Me: You know what I want? I want routine with you, I want waking up in the morning, with the sun shining or the rain pouring with you. I want home with you, too much late night TV and too much to drink with you. I want slow dancing in our living room. In our house, in our home, with you, I want you!

Erick: I miss you! There should be some dividends on transaction in Coinbase next week. You will get your weekly dividend I was informed.

Me: I look forward to it. I received my payout for my vacation time I had left when I retired but I do not want to invest it until you get here in case I need money for living expenses.

Erick: Hahaha my wife! Don't you know that you even need to invest it now more like a security for the future because it will be multiplying both weekly and monthly on Coinbase and on Lithium which you can always convert to cash than keep it at hand with no adding value then still spend it. I know you are wise and smart the sharpest arrow.

Me: So I put it in Coinbase as bitcoin?

Erick: Yes, Mrs. Andersen! How much did you receive Mrs. Andersen?

Me: I received five thousand

Erick: Alright my love, go ahead and do that invest it.

Me: I will my love

Erick: I know you will my arrow

Me: It is limiting me to one thousand increments at a time and 18 days hold time before transfers or withdrawal

Erick: Are you linking your card or your bank account?

Me: My bank account is linked to my account

Erick: Then maybe it is because that is your account online limit. You should increase your online limit or call your bank to assist you my love so that in the future too and maybe even when I am out for business and send you family up keep online you won't have a problem.

Me: I just bought one thousand for now till I can figure it all out.

Erick: Alright Mrs. Andersen. I have had a busy day first mom was moved to another ward.

Me: I love you and pray for you both, babe

Erick: I was hungry until your love satisfied me. I was thirsty until I drank from your heart. I was homeless until your heart found me. So now that I have you, I'll raise you above all others, I'll treat your lips with kind kisses as you caress my body with love. I'll return the favor into your bosom. I'll quench your thirst and satisfy your hunger all day long. I'll make the whole world testify for our love. And all eyes will see how elated we are in love. In the synagogue, I'll go worship with you and in the house of music, I'll dance joyfully with you. Come take my hand, my love and I will love you to the moon and back and I will always give praise to heaven that I found you. I was empty now I bow to the beauty that love fills and I have faith in this great love between us because you captured my heart away from all earthly worries. My destiny is to love you throughout all the ages. The bells of my heart toll with joy when my ears hearken to your voice. I see you in my dreams of taking your place in my home. I envision you walking towards my restless body, placing your kisses on my lips as the queen of my heart. Now I ask you so humbly that, you make my dreams come true for it is my greatest wish while I breathe, My beautiful Donna!

Me: I love you so much Mr. Andersen! How is your mother my love?

Erick: I am getting a specialist

Me: Yes, my love you told me that already. You said earlier that you moved her to a different ward but that is all. I did not know if it is good or bad news for her. I do not know anything unless you tell me, my love.

Erick: You are sweet, my love Thank you my love for looking after yourself enough for me. I am hoping this moves smoothly because I want you by my side. It makes me feel sad, honey what are you doing?

Me: Right now I take things one day at a time so I can plan accordingly. I am concentrating on what I can do to wrap things up here till you arrive.

Erick: You are such an amazing soul and I never knew you would love my family in such a way I'm moved to tears, my love. You need to grow also did you call the bank to take care of your online limit?

Me: No, I have not I will try tomorrow

Erick: Thank you so much my love for loving me the way you do I promise I will never love you less.

Erick: Good morning, my love I was doing some thinking last night and I was amazed how you have stood by me and I want to remind you that hard times are bound to come but they swiftly fade away with the winds if we both love unconditionally. With strength and patience, we'll see the finish line of our earthly race and wear the crowns as those deserving. We will sacrifice all that we can to enable our love to see the end of time because we believe in the fire of passion that burns in each other eyes. We'll give all that we can because we love wholeheartedly and make promises with the fear of God in our hearts. Take my hands because I am willing to love you till the trumpet sounds and this is my promise to you as long as I breathe.

Me: Good Morning, of course I am standing by you whether I am physically with you or not I have your back. I love you so much and I will be strong for you.

Erick: I love you baby! Have you called Coinbase?

Me: The bank said it is a safety precaution on my account so I just have to work around it. I bought another thousand last night, btw.

Erick: Alright Mrs. Andersen

Me: How are things there? How is Mom? Any change in her condition?

Erick: I am just getting here now give me a few minutes, my love

Me: Ok, keep me posted, my love

Erick: Honey, are you allergic to anything?

Me: Penicillin medication but no allergy to food

Erick: That's my soul, honey did you take care of the Coinbase?

Me: Yes, my love I told you I have made several purchases.

Erick: Alright my wife, I want when we meet we must have done all that we can individually. I love you so much and I will require your wallet to send for your weekly dividend tomorrow, OK?

Me: Ok, I will send it to you tomorrow in the morning

Erick: Alright my love, when will your deposits begin to mature so that I can alert them Mrs. Andersen?

Me: The holds are different on each bitcoin purchase starting with 13 days, babe

Erick: Alright my love, by Gods grace we should be together before then. My birthday is coming up and I want us to have a family thanksgiving time.

Me: That would be wonderful and we definitely have a lot to be thankful for!

Erick: That is correct my love. Have you ever done thanksgiving before?

Dorothy Harding

>**Me:** Yes, my love having family dinner and giving thanks. Is it different in the Bahamian culture, my love. I know Thanksgiving is different here in the states.
>**Erick:** This time around we are going to have a different type of celebration and we are going to the charity.

As of now I had invested over three thousand dollars in bitcoin and $1,300 had already been sent to him to invest in lithium. I received $15.15 and $24.02 in, supposedly, dividend payments from my initial investment. Then another $15.98 was received before I invested another $2,100. As of May 24, 2019, I invested $3,400 with dividend returns of only $55.15! He presented himself as a financial investor, so I felt no need for concern, but as things progressed, I became very suspicious of doing any additional investments simply because I received promises of additional dividend payments but never received any further after these payments. He had to show me good-faith payments to keep stringing me along in the scam. By now, it was June 2019, and with his family emergency and me in a holding pattern, I started to get concerned about the decisions I was making. Before, I was so busy working fulltime and moving and personal business, I really did not take time out to really absorb what was happening. I started to be concerned about what was going on.

>**Erick:** My wife because next month is investors promo on the lithium there is going to be about a 35% increase on dividends for pioneer investors and if you have introduced an investor you get another 15% on dividends. This is why I will advise you to take advantage of this window.
>**Me:** I still have the limits on my account and I was informed that they are not changing it is there for a security reason the only other thing is to maybe check blockchain to have a separate account if possible.
>**Erick:** That is a smart girl! I want you to see this as an opportunity that will even cover your time and you don't have to work for anyone, my love.
>**Me:** My husband, how are the boys? Are you able to spend some quality time with them?

> **Erick:** I am expecting them tomorrow or Sunday, babe
> **Me:** Good I will feel better when you are not all alone.
> **Erick:** I am preparing to head to hospital but I do not know if I want to wait for the boys I am waiting for them to confirm their arrival.
> **Me:** Are they flying alone?
> **Erick:** Oh yes, they flying alone and they had gone to NY.
> **Me:** I bet she will be happy to have all three of you with her
> **Erick:** My precious wife I love you and I want a kiss from you!
> **Me:** I always want a kiss from you, babe

Another series of six photos of him and the boys with their grandparents were sent. There was never a reason or warning when the photos were sent and, usually, a series of photos, most without quotes. By now I had gotten used to them, and sometimes I did not respond too much because what would I say? He had actually asked "Are you Ok?" when I did not respond to his pictures. He was acutely aware of my nonresponse to his pictures. It was all a part of the sale of his story; he had to make sure I believed in what he was selling me.

> **Erick:** We will make it up if possible, my love
> **Me:** How was your day? I am glad the boys made it there. Were those pictures taken today? you have a bad habit of not answering my questions you know!
> **Erick:** When do you think the pictures are taken my love?
> **Me:** I do not know that is why I am asking, Erick. I want to know if they are recent so I can change my wallpaper on my phone so I can keep the most current picture on my wallpaper, do you understand what I am saying?

He never did respond except to send me six more photos of him and the boys with their grandparents. During our relationship, as I am referring the scam as, he did not like for me to question him in any way. He picked and chose which questions to answer. He was always lovey dovey, but I did witness towards the end some anger from him when I made reference to ending our relationship.

Erick: My love I feel too tired my stepbrother is not in the country and it is not easy having to get Mom ready for today.
Me: Get some rest my love
Erick: My love I'm not feeling filled because my other half is not happy! What can I do to make up for the broken promises?
Me: I cannot change what has already happened this year all I can do is make sure my promises are kept in the future.
Erick: My love why are you exempting me? You do not want me to be with you in the future? My mom insisted she wanted to spend the day with the family because she felt the boys will miss their mother on a day like this my love and told me that she sincerely prays that you will be by my side for my birthday soon because she cannot wait to feel the presence of another woman that loves me and the boys before she passes on and I do not know why she said that and when I told her we still need her she says she prays that she will be strong enough to dance on our wedding day.
Me: I am sorry for what you are having to go through with your Mom, babe I pray for a swift recovery for her.
Erick: What a sweet woman you are! I am confirming the date of her surgery on Wednesday my love. Then I can breathe and come for you so we can proceed with our plans and go for a long vacation because we both need it.
Me: Your mother lives for you and those boys. I am glad you and the boys are spending some quality time with her today, she is fighting to be strong for you. Never doubt her pulling through the surgery so she can see us marry. You know a mother gathers strength from her children because that is her heart.
Erick: I will read out these words and show her my love
Me: She is preparing you for the future take this time to learn from her and abide by her wishes. Enjoy every moment you spend with her and let her guide you because in her eyes you are still her baby, Erick.

Erick: My wife, I love you. My body feels tired I wish we are together!

Me: Hopefully we will be together soon, babe

Erick: There is going to be a rise in bitcoin, my love. This is a great opportunity and I need you to take this opportunity. While I am taking care of things keep me updated ok?

Me: Always my love

Erick: My love every morning when I wake up and see your messages of love from your heart I give praises to my creator because when I carefully sought every corner of earth to find my love and I did make the first step of my leap of faith of finding my one and only soulmate and completeness by signing up on Zoosk and you showed up like a hopeful rainbow full of promises. You made me realize that love was to find me and when it did I knew in my heart that I was blesse amongst all men. I am glad you made that walk into my life for it erased the footprints of the searches and pain. You have made loving you so easy and thank you for making yourself available as a vessel from our creator to be perfect for me and a answer to all my prayers. My reality will begin when we going to make our vows of endless commitment to love and stand by each other through the remaining years as lovers and partners.

Me: I love you my sweetheart, more than you know

Erick: That is sweet and taking the right steps by faith also and that reminds me is there any progress with your Coinbase and Blockchain funding for your investment increase?

Me: There are still holds on the accounts and for security reasons they cannot be lifted and as far as Blockchain you have to set up a separate entity to transfer money in to the type of account. I cannot purchase directly through my Blockchain account yet.

Erick: You keep making me proud and confident in your sense of judgement my woman and I am proud of you daily. You are a mighty arrow and when will your funds begin to be ready?

Me: There are 2 holds one is 9 days and the other is 13 days from today, my love

It was always my understanding that he was a trained financial consultant, and during our conversations, he wanted me to learn about financial investing. We never discussed that this money was to be for his own personal funds. All the money I invested was just to be invested so I would never have to work when we were together. He seemed to be very articulate with knowledge of financial investments, even going as far as sending me online articles from Forbes.com and the *New York Times*, and when I clicked on these articles, they were legitimate articles. I had no doubts he knew what he was talking about as far as financial decisions. What I did not realize was he was using me to finance his own pockets, not ours!

Erick: My love Mom she first suffered from Spondylolistheses so this surgery will correct everything
Me: I have faith she will recover, my love she has a bad vertebrae in her back?
Erick: Thank you my wife it is costing me more than 2 million dollars.
Me: Is an orthopedic doctor doing the surgery? I had the surgery for the same condition in 2007
Erick: And he is doing robotic surgery
Me: It is easier surgery with less bleeding and quicker recovery. But that is a high price tag
Erick: This is one of the reasons I promised myself and you that we will not become an expensive liability to our children when we are very aged by looking after ourselves and also setting up a good financial foundation.
Me: Yes, my love I agree. But a good insurance helps too. Preventative maintenance is the key. that way you can catch it early and prevent extensive surgery sometimes.
Erick: Well insurance are people you enrich to invest your money, hahaha my wife
Me: Health insurance is what I was referring to and not life

insurance, babe

Erick: Oh my love, that's regardless honey it is most bitter in a long life value adding investment because even every insurance company investment to make profits and diverse into other multiple streams of income.

At this point I did not respond to this. I was very confused because, supposedly, he had lived in the states for years and was running a business. One of his businesses was selling medical instruments! How could he not know what health insurance was and how it worked? These responses started to confuse me because I am a logical-thinking person. I was unaware if The Bahamas had a healthcare system, but the fact he has worked for over twenty-plus years here in the States and did not understand the reference to health insurance did create red flags.

Erick: my wife?
Me: Yes, my love
Erick: I know my wife and I know my family is safe and my kingdom has the right queen with me and a virtuous woman in the family great things are happening.
Me: Yes, but it takes a strong unit to keep things running within a family. I promise to always work with you and advise you to the best of my knowledge and never stand against you we should always keep a united front.
Erick: I know you have the grace and you are chosen for me, I love you Donna Andersen
Me: I love you Erick Andersen, my love and soulmate
Erick: Thank you love
Me: How is everyone babe? Did they set a date for Mom's surgery?
Erick: They said everything being equal on the 12th my love.
Me: June 12th?
Erick: Yes, my love! You are disappointed?
Me: Yes, that means I won't see you for another month, babe
Erick: Is for two weeks my love. I feel even better now be-

cause I wasn't sure when the day would be.

Me: I'm sorry, I wished it would have been sooner, my love

Erick: I know my wife but it would have even been scheduled for a later day but insisted she wants to enjoy my birthday and with you in the family will mean everything to her.

Me: But I will not be there for your birthday, my love if her surgery is the 12th and your birthday is the 15th you will not be able to leave her to come here, babe.

Erick: Yes, so the 17th we are going to have family praise thanksgiving. How can that work my love? that is one of the issues I want to discuss with you.

Me: I don't know it is all in your hands I have no control over it.

Erick: My love, Who are you to me?

Me: I don't understand how I am supposedly to be there by the 17th why don't I just drive to Vegas and meet you at the house.

Erick: That is a great suggestion my love. How convenient is that for you my love.

Me: What date do you want to meet me there in Vegas?

Erick: The 14th my love should be best day. We will confirm the date, my love

Me: Yes, because I will leave om the 10th of June that way I can take breaks when needed.

Erick: Oh, my precious won't this not be too exhausting for you? What if we make plans to fly through and from?

Me: Fly through and from?

Erick: From your city to Vegas then from Vegas we leave to the Bahamas together

Me: What about my cats and the statue?

Erick: If I make plans for us to fly private jet we can have them along

Me: Sounds good to me just let me know times and date, my love

Erick: I love you baby

He had to deter me from making the drive to Vegas because I would have found out that he wasn't whom he appeared to be and no such home existed at the address he gave me. This proves how smooth he was at preventing me from realizing the truth. Later, I received a video call, and as always, when I tried returning the call, there was no answer.

Erick: My wife make sure you open wide your arms and embrace all the goodies, blessings, peace of mind, joy, happiness, laughter, forgiveness, grace and love that God has in store for you today. And also remember to share it with everyone that you come across today and always. because there is love in sharing just as you've shared your life with me. I love you so much more than you could ever imagine. I will return your call honey!
Me: What are you doing my husband?
Erick: I am responding to emails because I haven't because I was with Mom at the hospital and the boys have left,
Me: Where did the boys go, my love?
Erick: Going back to school my love. Their summer holiday begins June 17, 2019 to August 30, 2019 and they usually first spend some days before they finally come to meet me and we usually choose something fun to do together, Now, you should know that anything you suggest is welcomed because we are family now, babe
Me: I will make a suggestion when I get to know them and their interests. I am glad you got to spend Memorial Day with them and I am excited to meet them, my love.
Erick: Today, you need to realize that you are the best thing that ever happened to me. you are a blessing and your worth is greater than all the gold in the world. I can not compare how wonderful you are to my life and everyday I see reasons why we are just meant for each other. My darling I am stuck on you like a leech, not in a bad way but in a best way possible. You made me see that life is worth living when there is love. I am still battling with words to show how much you

me to me right now but could only come up with this. All I know is that our love story is going to be most exciting and passionate ever. I promise to love you forever so any suggestions for family fun is well accepted by you my queen.

Me: I promise to make suggestions for family fun in the future. I know you have a lot on your plate now to handle so when we are finally together we can find fun things to do as a family my love.

Erick: Honey, I have relatives I haven't seen in years and they are just coming to show love and support to Mom before her surgery.

Me: My love, that is awesome!

Erick: You are so amazing that you make me feel complete. I would not want any other person, I only want you in my life. I could not love anyone because my heart only wants you, my darling!

Me: I am so excited to see you soon and start our new life together as one

Erick: Something really sweet happened today, babe

Me: What my love?

Erick: A group of my mother's childhood friends came all the way from Georgetown to visit Mom and it was very emotional and I had not seen some of them for years now.

Me: I bet she is considered a much loved woman among her friends.

Erick: Yes, it gave me another peaceful feeling. Honey your wallet ID will be needed tomorrow Ok?

Me: I will send it to you in a little while, OK?

Erick: Please wait till in the morning, my love. It is usually better that way so that I will forward it myself directly OK?

Me: My love, I will use the Coinbase to receive it is easier.

Erick: My precious I love you and thank the Lord for bringing you into my life. As we enter into the sacred bonds of matrimony I promise to always love you in sickness as in health, in poverty or wealth, in sorrow and in joy, and to be faithful to you, my wife, so long as we both shall live.

Me: I promise the same to you my handsome soulmate and I love you with all my heart and soul.

Erick: I have no doubt whatsoever my queen. Honey I am preparing our shareholder file I need to know when will your other investment come ready?

Me: I checked earlier and it says 8 days both holds will be lifted, babe

Erick: I have an online seminar in the morning Mrs. Andersen and will share some knowledge with you.

Me: Ok, sounds good to me let me know I have some running to do in the morning. I got a call from the place I am boarding the cats and they are not eating.

Erick: Really, my wife. This is to show you that this is a trial phase to test our patience.

Me: Yes, this is definitely testing my patience! I need to go see if they will eat for me.

Erick: Nothing good comes easy. This is no fairy tale, babe. When we are finally together we have a story of our patience phase together.

Me: I hope we are together soon, my love

Erick: Good Morning, my mighty sharp blessed divine arrow, as I was thinking and meditating this morning of all I have been through it is clear to me now that everything in my life has led me to you, I think back on all my choices and consider even the bad ones blessed because if I had done even one thing differently that I might never had met you and about to become your husband and I vow to myself that as long as I breathe and see the break of a new day that I will enjoy myself in the loving soul in you because you have the most amazing soul in any woman I have met since my late wife passed away. I am a man that has enjoyed the love of angels in the form of women, first my mom then my late wife and now you and Wow I know that three is my lucky number so I am over excited with the future that lies ahead of us all we have to do is hold our hands together through this seed sowing phase if the fruits that we will enjoy in the future that is ahead of us my love.

> **Me:** Good morning, my love Here is my wallet ID you requested for the bitcoin.
> **Erick:** You are an amazing woman and I am proud to call you my wife.

He sent me a video about new technology from Michio Kaku about computer chips and digitalized technology; it was five minutes long. Michio Kaku is an American theoretical physicist, futurist, and popularizer of science. He is a professor of theoretical physics in the City College of New York and CUNY Graduate Center; this is according to Wikipedia.

> **Erick:** My love please I need you to check your wallet again and resend it to me and I want to assure you that I am praying with you that nothing bad has happened with the cats, Ok?
> **Me:** Here is my wallet address for bitcoin again
> **Erick:** Good girl, I have sent it across my love
> **Erick:** My love, you know I use biometric remote security system in our house but my brother said he might be coming back from the Atlantic if he comes before Mom's surgery he will pass by and bring your things to the house and come with you also here.
> **Me:** I thought you were coming here to get me? How is he coming here? I am totally confused!
> **Erick:** Yes, my love I am coming but I am worried you might get impatient
> **Me:** I am not impatient. I am unhappy because every single decision I made so far has come with a price in this decision to be together. I am sorry but I have my hands full right now and so do you. I just need to know what is going on so I can plan accordingly.
> **Erick:** I love you so much, my wife. I promise to challenge you to be everything I know you can be, to never be trapped in despair, to always see in yourself what I see in yourself what I see in you, an amazing woman, a sharp edged arrow my wife for whom I will always feel the greatest pride and

admiration.

Me: I received the deposit on the bitcoin, my love

Erick: Have you received your retirement fund?

Me: No, I tried calling but have no answers it should be another 3 weeks

Erick: You see that even this delay is giving us time to tighten every ends because we are going to have uninterrupted time in years.

Me: I might have received a letter on retirement but all my mail is supposed to be going to the Vegas address. I know I have several checks going there like the deposit on my apartment is being mailed there too.

Erick: I am sorry no one is home there, my love

Me: It will be safe in the mailbox there won't it?

Erick: Yes, my love only our family has access to the mailbox

Me: Then I am not worried then, babe

Erick: I love you baby

Me: I love you more, babe

Erick: I'm sorry I took some pain killers when I got home from hospital and it got me fuzzy so I slept as soon as I got home.

Me: Why are you in pain, my love?

Erick: I have not rested, my love

Me: I wish there was something I can do to help you at least ease your mind. When do you think you will be here I need to know so I can board the cats at a different place for now?

Erick: Oh, honey please let me confirm this weekend. I want to be very sure of the date I will arrive so that we will be on point with our plans.

Me: Ok, my love let me know as soon as possible because I have to make a decision to give to the animal hospital that is boarding them now.

Erick: Alright my love can we get a date for now then like the 14th? Because my desire is to be with you and the same time I don't want to give a date and come before or after that but to leave the date open if that is the best choice.

It was getting close to his birthday, and he had already blown me off on two other occasions on when he was to arrive. May 11, 2019, and Memorial Day. Now there was June 14th closing in as the next date. He had to keep stringing me along because there was more money to be had. He was not done with me yet, and he had to continue to convince me to keep hanging on to his promises of arrival to be with me.

>**Me:** I called and told them I would pick them up by the 15th of June but could be sooner if plans change
>
>**Erick:** My love do you know when things are meant to be, there is nothing that can hinder the reality. If humans have been created for each other, nothing can stop them except god. This is my greatest believe and I really mean it. I mean this special reality called love for you. I want to show you to the world that you are the best woman on earth. you are the coolest love that everyone will like to have forever. Thank God I am so lucky to have you. To be sincere, if I am presented with the world and all that it contains of ornaments and treasure before me I will go with you with you in heaven that is better than this small life. I want to be your angelic husband in an angelic world. In a beautiful world where there will be no death forever that is where I want to be with you. I love everything about you and you may not understand the pearl of love you are. You are the best for me and you are the most gorgeous lover I have seen ever. I love you to the last end of my heart. I love you my darling.
>
>**Me:** I love you and your beautiful love letter fill my heart with such warmth, my husband
>
>**Erick:** What are you doing my darling?
>
>**Me:** Reading my love, I had a busy day. What are you doing?
>
>**Erick:** It's another book now tell me how it is, honey when I come home I respond to mails from my staffs and catch up some other work I can do from here. I can't wait to pass the

phase and be with you and family in your health.

His love letters were immaculate, but he slipped, especially when tired, and his wording was more of him, the true scammer. Would you consider the last text that of a man who has spent over twenty-five years here in the United States working and starting a financial investment company and living here in the States? Most of our conversations were premeditated or well thought of. He answered only the questions he had answers to immediately and mostly never answered ones he didn't, as you will see as our conversations continue.

> **Me:** I spent over an hour at the vets office regarding the cats. The vet said they are fine but very unhappy because of the situation and I am very upset. I spent $1400 on boarding and vet bills and not working this will become a problem soon. I understand your predicament but you must understand mine too, babe
>
> **Erick:** I am sorry my wife, I am truly my love. I know this is all because of Mom's health. If it wasn't for me you won't be in this phase but I can promise you it's going to end soon and comes from the love I will shower you and care for you.
>
> **Me:** This was my decision I should have waited and made better decisions. This waiting is not in my best interest. You have to do what you need to do to take care of your mother. I am giving it one more week that is my limit then I have to make decisions.
>
> **Erick:** My love please let's not hope it even gets to that! We need to be together in prayers now. I think this was the start of the turning point for me where I realized maybe I made a very bad decision to be with him and give up my life. The broken promises and uncertainty was not sitting well with me. The doubts of everything started creeping in and I was very worried. He had to scramble to keep me in line at this point.
>
> **Me:** I pray constantly Erick and its all I can do because I don't want to look at the alternative.

Erick: Thank you my love and I can feel the effects of your prayer. Pay love just like sunshine, I have found you shining in my heart. Like the blossom of love, happiness and endless joy. I have been given all it takes to be yours now and forever. You are the best in this world for me. You are so much important to me. I love you like never before and will do every minute of my life. I care for you and I need you and will do no matter the condition. To the one I have been searching for all my life, don't forget that you are the one my heart has chosen. You are the only true love the Love has so far sent to me. I want you to wipe your tears because no one can take me away from you. No one can stop me from loving you. I will be there always. I will make sure I put a smile on your face. I will never stop loving you until the end of time. To you my heart will always be for, to you my heart will never stop loving. Just be rest assured that you belong to me. You are the most wonderful love of my life. That angel I cannot stop loving forever. I miss you and I dedicate my heart for you so it will be easy to do almost everything for you. To the one I cherish the loveliest moments spraying love on you. I love you my darling and sweet angel.
Me: I love you too, my soulmate
Erick: My love, I will make up all this time to you
Me: My love, I can only pray things will work out for my cats and your mother's health.
Erick: I love you Donna you have the sweetest soul. You will never regret your decision of choosing me.
Me: I love you, Erick
Erick: I love you my wife, how is your health my love?
Me: I am good, babe How is my beautiful husband doing? You keeping your mother entertained?
Erick: I miss you so much I am on my way to the hospital now, my wife
Me: I am reading a book it is a spiritual guidebook on how to find inner peace within yourself.

Erick: There is one I read some years ago. The title is The Purpose Driven Life when I remember the author I will tell you.
Me: I just was on Barnes and Noble website and it shows Rick Warren is the author who wrote The Purpose Driven Life: What Am I is this the book you were talking about?
Erick: Wow yeah my love. Rick yes, he's the author. Have you read it before?
Me: No, babe I just looked up the title you gave me because I was on the website as we were speaking. Is it good?
Erick: You are an amazing soul. Can I ask you a question?
Me: You can ask me anything, babe
Erick: What age would you wish you passed away?
Me: I am hoping to live a long life but there has to be a quality of life that is what truly matters.
Erick: My wife this is deep and I want us to continue and conclude with prayers.
Me: Yes, my love because it is all in God's hands anyway we have no idea when we are going to pass away. But we have a lot to pray for and thank god for because we have a lot of good years ahead of us and a beautiful life to lead.
Erick: Do you have an idea of how you want to leave?
Me: You do not have a choice on how you want to leave. I want to leave surrounded by love ones and a chance to say goodbye to them. That is my wish but ultimately it is all in God's hands.
Erick: You shall not die untimely but declare the glory of our creator in Jesus name.
Me: I have no intention of leaving this earth without a fight. I have a strong will to live and have not fulfilled my purpose here on earth yet. I feel the best is yet to come that is my belief.
Erick: You know what is amazing my wife? We have the same vision and I want to hold hands with you now and forever.
Me: Thank you and I hope we have a long happy life together.

Erick: My love some of Mom's church deaconess group came to the house and I took them to the hospital honey to see her.
Me: That is good, babe
Erick: You know I want to get you to be a shareholder investor and also my partner, not just my wife, because I believe in multiple streams of income and I want you to adopt the idea.
Me: Yes, my love
Erick: Do you know when your funds will be ready?
Me: 4 more days and all holds will be lifted
Erick: Alright my wife then we can take it from there ok. I want to be involved to bring you on board personally. Do you know the advantages?
Me: You will have to educate me on that, my love
Erick: Yes, I will so that even when I am not home you are working comfortably from anywhere making money by understanding boldness and foresight.
Me: Ok, my love
Erick: I love you so much, my wife. Did you eat?
Me: Yes, I ate earlier my love. Did you eat my husband?
Erick: Not yet my wife but I have ordered for a boneless grilled fish which I have the appetite for.
Me: Lean protein is good for you and it is considered brain food but you should eat some veggies to make it a balanced meal.
Erick: Thanks, my love I enjoy a lot of that. Honey summer holidays for the boys begins June 17 – August 30th did I tell you?
Me: Yes, you did are they going to be there for your birthday?
Erick: Honey we are all going to be together as a family and I will make sure of that. We will have all two months together then you and I will have our vacation if that is ok with you.
Me: Yes, I agree that is good because the boy's needs should come first we will have plenty of time to spend together and

it will give your mother time to heal also if the boys stay with us this summer.
Erick: I love you my best friend. Did I tell you when her surgery is set?
Me: Yes, you told me the 12th, my love
Erick: My wife I am on my way to the airport to get some relatives they want to be around her before the surgery.
Me: That's good! I am so happy you won't be alone for her surgery, babe
Erick: I love you my queen. My wife what time do you think we can do your other transaction tomorrow so that I can plan myself and with the transaction I am assigning on processing a shareholding investment for you in the lithium.
Me: Yes, my husband anytime is good for me babe
Erick: Alright my wife. I think lunch time is best
Me: Ok, my love. How was Mom's surgery, babe?
Erick: My love today's surgery was successful she is old and weak so they are monitoring her and will continue in the morning.
Me: That is normal my love. With her age she will take longer to heal and I am so glad my prayers were answered and it was a success.
Erick: Thank you, babe. Now we are getting closer my wife

I kind of missed the red flag that he was vague on the information on her surgery but brought up the money I was investing on the day of his mother's surgery. You would have thought he would have provided me with more details on the surgery to sell the story better. He only brought up his mom's illness or surgery to pacify me when I asked about her. But when it came to talking about my investment, he would go into more detail.

Erick: My wife here is my wallet and my advise is you should increase your fund as much as you can Because there is a huge increase. Here is my wallet ID. My love?
Me: Ok, I just sent it let me know the transaction was con-

firmed.

Erick: My wife, how much did you send through?

Me: $2093 that was minus fee

Erick: Alright honey, you didn't make it the $5000 you intended to?

Me: No, I had to spend $1400 on boarding my cats and I had to pull my car from online sale and pay car insurance on it because I need it till you get here plus; I have other bills. With this delay in me leaving here I have to wait to do any other investment. I should have waited to do any investment until you came here anyway.

Erick: I love you baby! I have put together you're filing you will get your weekly dividend this weekend or Monday.

Me: We can discuss it when you arrive here. I need to know when you are coming so I can arrange to pick up the cats at the boarding place. They are closed Sundays so I will need to pick them up Saturday if needed. Ok, my love?

Erick: I love you my wife and I miss you honey. I feel sad but happy because I know our marriage will happen now in a bigger way because the journey of our relationship has made us stronger and created a deeper feeling toward each other.

Me: I just wish we were together during this tough time in our relationship and I pray everything works out in the end.

Erick: Yes, my love

Me: Good morning, Birthday boy I hope today is as beautiful as you are. I cannot wait to wrap my arms around you and show you how much I love you!

Erick: My wife I love you. You have brought such joy to my life. Thank you for loving me as I am and taking me into your heart. I promise to walk by your side forever and to love, help and encourage you in all that you do. I will take the time to talk to you and listen to you and care for you. Through all the changes of our lives, I will be there for you always as a strength in need, a comfort in sorrow, a counselor in difficulty, and a companion in joy. Everything I am and every-

Scammed in America

thing I have is yours now and forever more. This is my promise to you.
Me: My beautiful soulmate, Happy Fathers Day, I am so glad to hear from you but you have not been keeping me up to date on what is going on. I know you are busy but if I am going to have to sustain till you come I need to know what is going on. You promised me we would be together by tomorrow and I feel like it is not happening at this point. I am going to have to obtain a job if I stay here much longer because I have no income coming in till I receive my retirement check and at this point I do not know when you will be here or not. You seem to forget the predicament you have put me in.
Erick: I'm sorry my wife. I'm going to give you every update but I want to have a conclusive word because too many things are in my hand at this minute and I am handling one at a time for effectiveness.

This became the beginning of the end of my belief in him. I started to lose faith in the belief that he was coming at all. I could feel the strain of everything I had given up and the sacrifices I had made. This was mid-June by now, and no solid answers, only excuses came from him.

Me: Did you get to at least see or talk to the boys today?
Erick: They are coming back tomorrow, my wife
Me: That is good you will get to see them, I wish I could be there too!
Erick: I miss you, my wife. I am sorry love everything is going to be alright. Mom is set to recover next week, my darling
Me: I wish her all the love and hope she recovers. How are you holding up? This has been hard on you too. I just worry when you don't keep me informed for long periods of time babe.
Erick: I love you my wife, you make every day blissful. I went to do some grocery shopping for The orphans and went to

deliver it with some of my relatives.

Me: That is sweet my love. Is there an orphanage there?

Erick: Yes, my wife with 57 kids and I told them we are going to come back!

Me: Wow, can I come with you when you go?

Erick: Can? That is an understatement because you are the one next to me. It is like a must but I'd rather not use the word must.

Me: You know what my first job was? Teaching arts and crafts to under privileged children at age 14. I have a soft spot for unloved kids and animals, babe.

Erick: Oh Wow! The boys are with me now

Me: That's good, babe

Erick: The boys said they have a surprise for you honey but I honestly do not know what it is.

Me: That is sweet, my love. I hope they like cats.

Erick: Yeah, they do my love. They have some friends coming to see them tomorrow. They seem very excited.

Me: That is good, babe

Erick: Soon I know we are going to create new beautiful family memories together **Me:** I pray soon, my love

(Ten more photos were texted to me; most were of vintage cars and him and the two boys.)

Me: What are those photos a dealership or museum? My love

Erick: Is our dealership my love. I bought the boys to show them the progress and to familiarize them with it. This is just one of the investments I have set up for them. It is the first time I am bringing them here.

Me: You are a wonderful father, Erick

Erick: You are an amazing woman and I will never trade you. I'm asking the lawyer to make a memorandum.

Me: I have already committed to you, my love I hope you don't want to trade me in already.

Erick: Never! I have been looking for you now that I have found you. I will groom you to bring out the best of you for us.

On quite a few occasions, he made mention of grooming me or teaching me to live in his world; this should have been a red flag for me, but I also took it as adapting to his culture or way of life. In reality, it was meant for keeping me in line and providing him with a constant stream of income.

> **Me:** I cannot wait to be together with you, babe
> **Erick:** I know my wife as much as I would for you. My love how have you been surviving?
> **Me:** Every day is harder without being by your side and I hope that is soon
> **Erick:** Your Mother in law she wants to be ready for our wedding and doesn't want you to meet her sick. She wants to be up and ready for you and she is fighting to do that for you.
> **Me:** She does not have to be strong for me because she is already is a strong woman. I am looking for all the things she can teach me about your family traditions. That is what I am most looking forward to. Tell her I will continue to pray for her and hope to see her soon.
> **Erick:** I am more than blessed to have found you, Donna!
> **Me:** Have you heard of Libra? It's a new cryptocurrency Facebook is launching
> **Erick:** Yes, my love. You are really smart! It is the yellow crypto. Hahaha, I love this woman.
> **Me:** Yellow crypto? You have a lot to teach me, babe
> **Erick:** I am proud of you and I will teach you how to trade from home so you can be making money
> **Me:** I am eager to learn from you, Mr. Andersen
> **Erick:** I miss you, my love
> **Me:** I always miss you, babe
> **Erick:** Yes, we will be getting closer to being together. Your dividends will be ready tomorrow ok? this will be your weekly I just got notification by mail.

Me: Thanks for the notification, babe I never received another so called dividend on my so called investment in lithium again as you will see moving forward things changed.
Erick: Your in-law is responding well to treatment and should be expected back to the recovery ward soon.
Me: That is good news!
Erick: My wife we are going to be together soon.
Me: I am looking forward to that day, babe
Erick: What is your stance on movie ratings? Are there movies you will or will not watch because of the ratings? What are some of your all-time favorite movies?
Me: I really do not pay attention to moving ratings at all. If I see a movie trailer I like I go to see the movie. I don't like horror movies I mostly like action or comedy type of movies. I like documentaries too. Ratings are for people who have children who need to filter what their children see.
Erick: Do you feel it is appropriate for parents to censor children's reading? Are there any books you would not let your children read? Are there any books you feel are inappropriate for adults to read?
Me: I think there are things children should be censored on as far as book content. They should be given books based on age appropriate material. Especially violence and sexual content no child should have this information at a young age. As far as adults and inappropriate reading material well they are adults let them make their own decisions.
Erick: Do you agree that the husband is the head of the family? Why or why not? What does it mean for the husband to be the head of family?
Me: We both grew up where our perspective fathers were head of the family. Times have changed and even though those values we grew up with are still used in families it is not necessarily the norm any more. I think it should be individually decided per each couple on how they wish to co-exist as a couple or as a family unit. I think it helps to have a united

front on all decisions made by families.

Erick: You are an intelligent woman and I am most blessed to have you. We will also talk about more issues on my observations on the boys and your opinion.

Me: Ok, my love

Erick: Do you feel that the whole family should clean house together or should it just be the wife's job? Would you ever want to have a maid or do you ever feel that is wasteful?

Me: I am a well-trained cleaner I use to do it commercially. Besides if it is not done right I will redo it. Maid services are good especially for heavy cleaning but I do expect everyone to pick up after themselves.

Erick: Would you consider yourself to be a messy person or a neat freak? How much mess can you tolerate by others that you live with?

Me: I like to be organized, clothes folded neatly, shoes lined up and dishes cleaned and put away. I can tolerate some mess but eventually I will straighten it up.

Erick: Do you think it is more important to let the Lord make decisions for you or to make them on your own? How big of a role should the Lord's counsel play in both small and large decisions?

Me: The lord plays a role in all decisions especially important ones. If I make a large decision I pray on it and hope God guides me in the right direction.

Erick: Do you believe that marriage can be a happy and fulfilling relationship? Or do you fear it will be fraught with difficulty?

Me: Yes, I would not dedicate myself to a person if I felt otherwise. Marriage is a constant work with your spouse on common goals as one unit. A good marriage should be happy and fulfilling for both. Yes, there will be difficult times along with good times. That is life and how well you support one another and comfort them only strengthens your marriage.

Erick: Do you like to set goals for yourself? How are you at accomplishing goals that you set? Do you write them down or just think of them? Do you tell them to others or keep them private.

Me: Yes, I have set personal goals for myself. I am a driven person but I allow myself a fail safe also. I generally keep all my personal goals to myself because after all they are personal goals not public goals. Sometimes they get achieved and sometimes they are changed for different reasons.

Erick: What are some of your long term and short term goals?

Me: Lead a happy healthy life is my main long term goal! I would like to learn Spanish and be financially comfortable to be able to perform more random acts of kindness something the world lacks right now. To stop working so hard and appreciate the little things in life and to travel to Europe are some of my short term goals.

Erick: Do you think it is Ok for a married person to have a friend of the opposite sex? If so how much contact should be allowed? Only talking at work? Going out to lunch? Phone calls?

Me: Yes, if you are comfortable and secure in your marriage or relationship whether your friends are of the opposite sex or gender neutral it does not matter. Work. Lunch or phone calls are appropriate but meeting after hours on personal time or in hotels and private residence should be have a good explanation. I am not a insecure or jealous person but then my ex-husband carried on a affair with a mutual friend for a couple of years so I am aware of infidelity within a marriage.

Erick: Awww, What have I done to deserve you, my love. Do you think it is important to eat dinner together as a family or do you prefer to let each family member eat when it is convenient for them?

Me: I grew up in a working class family where the father worked all day and the mother stayed home and took care of the house and children. Dinner time was the same time and all were expected to appear or no dinner. But I realize that now especially with two adults working in the family that sometimes having dinner together regularly in not normal but I would expect some time during the week to have the family all sit down together to not only have a meal together but to catch up on each persons individual life and have some precious family time together.

Erick: When you are in a bad mood, do you prefer to be left alone or comforted? Do you like to have someone brainstorm to help you solve problems or do you prefer just a listening ear and understanding without the other person volunteering solutions?

Me: I love a good ear and then someone to give me an unbiased opinion. I love to be comforted when I am hurting whether it be physical or emotional pain.

Erick: Do you find it difficult to apologize or is it easy for you? Do you think it is important for Both people to apologize after an argument or should only one apologize? Do you think couples should take turns apologizing or should it just be the person who is at fault? Do you think it is important to be the first person to apologize after an argument?

Me: I have no problem apologizing or saying I am sorry and admitting when I am wrong. I am a truly honest and straight forward person. I will say I am sorry I hurt your feelings, I am sorry you cannot see my point of view and I am sorry to argue with you but if you don't disagree you do not learn to see the others point of view. If you do not apologize it can leave hard feelings and resentment between couples. In the end a good relationship is give and take and you both should give in to the other if they are passionate about the issue and learn to let the argument go. If I agree with everything then I am not being honest with you so if I strongly disagree with you I will take your opinion in consideration.

Erick: My love, would you consider yourself to be primarily logical or emotional? Which do you use to make decisions? Do you find yourself reacting to situations using gut instinct or logical thought processes?

Me: I have an unusual analytical logical mind. If I become upset it can get emotional so I really try not to make any decisions when I am emotional. I can shut down my emotions especially under duress and think logical because that is needed. It may seem cold but in emergencies a clear head is what is needed not an emotion. I think first gut instincts are a warning to not proceed or to proceed with caution. Gut instinct super cedes logic on most all occasions and definitely important ones.

Erick: You are an intelligent woman and I am proud to be your man. What is your definition of love? Do you feel there are different types of love?

Me: My definition of love between a man and woman is heartfelt happiness, euphoric sweetness deep inside your soul. There are different types of love and different degrees. Example: Love of life is different then love of another person. Love of your significant other is different than love of a child and Love of family is different of love of a friend. Depending on the person in your life is the depth of love for one another.

Erick: Wow my love, you marvel me!

Me: You are sweet my love

Erick: You have Mrs. Andersen on your name tag from heaven

Me: We were meant to meet in this lifetime.

Erick: Mom said she is feeling a presence and a hand holding her

Me: That is her guardian angel watching over her and I am glad it is bringing her some peace.

Erick: My love, has your money come through? How are you coping?

Me: I am still waiting to hear back from Human Resources because they say they mailed my info to the Vegas address so I cannot access my online account. I was able to reroute my security deposit on my apartment here I should receive it soon. I have no idea about my mail till you come get me and I get to Vegas.

Erick: Please update me my wife!

Me: Are we going to be in Vegas for the 4th of July?

Erick: Yes, we should my love. Because all things being equal I am just waiting for final Doctor's report on Monday.

Me: Good, my love! I am praying for a positive outcome. Please keep me informed it is important to me too.

Erick: Amen, my wife What are you thinking of?

Me: My future, babe

Erick: My wife, what about your future that doesn't include me.

Me: I have considered you in my future but I am very worried now. My life hinges upon others decisions that I have no control over.

Erick: If I was in your shoes, I will feel the same way, my love. But we have to fight together.

Me: I miss you and I hope my luck changes soon!

Erick: The care and love you bestowed upon me are captivating and I wish I could repay you someday. I know that no amount of money would be enough to repay your unconditional love for me. So I will spend a lifetime to cherish and love you with every breath in me till the end of time. I hope that will cover it all. You know that I love you right? Well, I do! Always have and always will!

Me: I love you too and hope to see your handsome face soon!

Erick: Mom is recovering and I know she will be more delighted

Me: That is good babe. I wish her well and a speedy recovery. I know you are too busy for us right now. Contact me when you have some free time.

Erick: You are the best, my wife!

The 4th of July had come and gone, and no updates on what was going on had really caused me a big disappointment. I am starting to struggle to keep my head above water and wondered if this relationship was ever going to move forward. I started to notice inconsistencies in the information he was giving me.

> **Erick:** My love, I know soon we will all be together celebrating every day in love.
> **Me:** I am hoping this situation improves and hope it is all uphill from here, babe
> **Erick:** I have no doubt about your commitment to our life and I will never let you down. Now let's do some family planning. Did you check how much you can come up with, my wife.
> **Me:** I cannot access nothing, I have no job and no permanent address and no collateral for a loan at this point. I am considering job hunting now just so I can survive here because me leaving here is undetermined at this time!
> **Erick:** My wife and you have not received your retirement fund yet?
> **Me:** No, I was supposed to receive my first check in July but so far, no check! I am very upset over this situation. I should never have given up my job and home without a fail safe and I am starting to feel the repercussion of my decisions.
> **Erick:** I am sorry, my wife that is ridiculous you have to wait for your retirement. I realize I should never have invested any money without having a roof over my head first.

All the promises he made never came through. I feel a lot of doubt and had started to pull together a resume to start job hunting because things were not going well for me financially. He sent two photos to me of him and some other men.

> **Erick:** This are some of my senior staff, They all said since I had not celebrated my birthday and I'm Busy with family they all planned to spend the weekend with me.
> **Me:** That's nice
> **Erick:** I was not ready but they planned it and my manager

just called me that they were at the Airport.

Me: I hope you have a wonderful time together, Erick.

Two more pictures of him sitting next to a pool with a glass of champagne in his swim trunks were sent. I was really disappointed that he had not made arrangements for me, especially after all the broken promises.

Me: Nice pictures

Erick: I got a paid massage for the weekend from my staff, honey. I feel refreshed.

Me: That's nice of them, babe

Erick: You sound jealous, my love. They said I look exhausted my wife and they decided to surprise me. I know you wish we were together. Don't worry we will that I assure you my love.

Me: No, I am not jealous but I do not understand why we are not together!

Erick: My love, I am waiting for Mom to be discharged honey. I thought you knew that and she needs to get back on her feet.

Me: No, you do not tell me nothing and you do not answer all of my questions when I ask!

Erick: My mother said she wants to be on her feet to receive you. Didn't I also tell you she is recovering from a 3D physiotherapy?

Me: No, you have not informed me of any of these things. You should really look back at all of your texts to me!

Erick: Oh, my love. I thought I have been telling all these things to you. I think I told you about her pains and how we chose 3D therapy.

Me: No, I am not kidding you. I have barely spoke with you and mostly briefly and maybe once a day and always late at night.

Erick: My love, Mom has been moved to the full recovery ward.

Me: That is good! Is she still doing physical therapy?

Erick: Yes, my wife. It's been very tight for me lately honey
Me: Tight schedule?
Erick: The boys are now with me and Mom is still in the hospital
Me: I know you are busy, my love. Just know I am here waiting for you!
Erick: I have so many ways to make it up to you my wife. Honestly speaking I need to be in Hong Kong and Japan for the lithium shareholders summit and I must be there with you.
Me: when is the Summit?
Erick: It is from August 30th – September 6th
Me: That is coming up soon, babe!
Erick: Yes, my wife I know! So, I need you to begin to get ready so that when we are together we won't have to rush preparing.
Me: What do I need to do to prepare. My love?
Erick: I will get all necessary information and update you, OK?
Me: Ok, my love
Erick: Do you use WhatsApp?
Me: No, what is WhatsApp?
Erick: It is an app that our boys and some of our staff introduced me to.

As of this point, we had texted on Zoosk, then switched to our personal cell phone messaging, then to Viber app. Now he was wanting to move to WhatsApp. WhatsApp is a Facebook app that is highly used by scammers so they may keep all their "client" or victims on the same app so as to keep track of who they are talking to and what they have said. It is also easy for another scammer to pick up on the conversation and to take over because, in most cases, you are not talking to only one scammer but multiple. I noticed Erick on occasion would repeat himself, especially on his love letters, and say things like "Remember I told you about this." It would answer a lot of questions I had as to why he never would answer a particular question I had asked prior.

Me: Like a messenger app?
Erick: Yes, look it up my wife
Me: So you want to use it instead of Viber?
Erick: Yes, lets try my wife
Me: Ok, I installed it and sent you a message.

I installed the app and sent him a link; it said this chat was with a business account. Messages and calls are end-to-end encrypted. No one outside of this chat, not even WhatsApp, can read or listen to them. I think by being a business app, it meant any of his associates had access to his conversations. I have not been able to get WhatsApp to verify this, but at the beginning, it said Erick registered as a business account, but WhatsApp hasn't verified their name yet. This was proclaimed on the message from the app.

Erick: Hello my love. Type yes if you get this
Me: Yes
Erick: I love you baby. I think this is cool
Me: How is your mother, babe?
Erick: She started trying to make conversations and she was just making signs before.
Me: I was not aware she was not communicating well, my love
Erick: She wasn't my love
Me: I am glad she is doing better.
Erick: My love you will need investor attendees form for our trip.
Me: Where do I get the form?
Erick: You have to purchase it from them even committed
Me: Is there a website? Purchase from who?
Erick: This year my love it is strictly by invitation so I will apply for you then you will pay by bitcoin with Your reference code.
Me: How much bitcoin will it cost?
Erick: $2300 my love

I did not respond. I had a strange feeling about this. I think my gut instinct kicked in, and I dropped the subject entirely for that reason. He had never mentioned anything about me paying for anything regarding this trip. Every conversation prior mentioned him footing the bill for this trip. I was stunned when he asked for me to pay for an attendee's form.

> **Erick:** What are you doing?
> **Me:** I am doing so cleaning babe. How are you today?
> **Erick:** He is feeling like the most loved man alive because of your loving.
> **Me:** I am glad you are happy, Erick
> **Erick:** As I woke up this morning the sunlight was rushing through the room and it lit up every dark corner that there was. There was this feeling of inexplicable joy in my heart and I knew it at the moment that I needed to tell you just how much I love you. Forgive me, for I am not a writer, and may not know the best way and the best words to use. All I do know is that I love you and I want to spend the rest of my life with you. You have given me so much joy and and unconditional·love that I am quite sure that I am the luckiest man alive on the face of the earth. So, all I ask of you is to continue loving me and I promise you that I shall do everything in my power to take care of you and love you till the end of time.
> **Me:** I love you too! My beautiful poet and soulmate, Mr. Andersen
> **Erick:** Are you ready for our trip?
> **Me:** I have no worries yet. I will be ready when you get here.
> **Erick:** Good Girl! I believe in you. When are you planning to buy the form?
> **Me:** I got to see where I can get the money, babe. Without a paycheck for two months it is a struggle. I do not have $2300, my love.
> **Erick:** I will take care of the trip and other things my love. My hands are a bit tight that is why I am asking you to pay

for the form yourself.
Me: I need every penny I have to survive and I gave up everything to be with you and you should have known I do not have this money for this form. If I knew when you would be here I can sell my car but not until you arrive. Otherwise I cannot attain this money for this form.
Erick: Alright my love, I will tell you when to go handle that.
Me: How are you doing my love? Are you getting enough sleep? Are you eating well?
Erick: Honey I will when we are together. I miss you, babe
Me: I miss you, too
Erick: Honey, I think you will need to get your form next week, Ok?
Me: So I need to sell my car next week? We discussed this that I would sell my car when you arrived and use that money for the bitcoin form.
Erick: Yes, I will give you exact date my love
Me: Ok, my love

He wanted me to just send him $2,300 in Bitcoin for the form, but because of prior investments and no income coming in, I refused to sell my car till he would arrive. I stood firm on my decision and still do not regret that. I had to decide that I had to survive till he actually showed up as promised.

Erick: Mom is feeling life today
Me: Is she regaining her strength? I pray for her daily.
Erick: Yes, my wife and I miss you. You are a beautiful woman and I can see you are ready for us.
Me: I miss you, Erick
Erick: You are my reality and I cannot imagine a world without you. You are my heart robber.
Me: You are sweet my love
Erick: I will give praise to the heavens because I have found you. Because I believe you were sent from above to fill my heart with joy and from the way I feel deep inside when I vi-

sualize our future together my heart is filled with joy because all one is my arrow, my partner, my soulmate, my co-pilot together we sailing to out destined desire. So hold my hands because I will never let you out of my eyesight.

Me: I love you, babe

Erick: Thank you for believing in us and in our love and I Erick Andersen want to promise you on the grave of my late wife and my late dad that I will never let you down. I will never allow anything to come between us and my feelings for you will never change negatively but always growing positively to better you in every aspect of your life because I know that the best of you I will bring out the best of you in my world to enjoy and I know that two heads are better than one so you can rest assure that your opinions will always count in every decision I make individually and also collectively. Now I am no longer a single man but a man committed to share the rest of my living with such an amazing angel in the body of a beautiful woman who was specially curved and set aside to complete this remaining journey of my life. Now that I have found you I will be with you even after the end of time my precious woman.

Me: I love you Mr. Andersen and I cannot wait to see what life has in store for us.

Erick: You complete me, my wife. I love you

Me: How is your mother today? Are you keeping her entertained?

Erick: She is able to talk more today

Me: That is awesome babe! I am so overjoyed she is able to communicate better.

Erick: Thank you my love. Now we're meant to be because we have been through everything that tried to make us believe otherwise. I love you will you marry me?

Me: Of course, I will marry you when the time comes and we are finally together.

Erick: I will always bless the day that I met you. I will be with you soon, my wife

Me: I hope so my love

Erick: Do you think each spouse has a right to demand sexual intimacy from the other? Who should decide how often a couple is sexually intimate? Who should initiate intimacy?

Me: I think if you are open and honest with each other intimacy should never be a problem. That includes being open to the others needs and desires sexually. It does not matter who initiates the intimacy or how often as long as both agree to satisfy one another needs and desires. That is the part of marriage that should always be sacred between the two lovers.

Erick: What is your opinion on gun control?

Me: I think there should be stricter regulation on gun control. I believe if you qualify you have a right to bear arms but you do not have a right to take another life because you own a gun. we live in a unstable environment and there is so much hate we don't need firearms in the wrong hands. No one should own a bump stock or automatic assault weapon. The military are the only ones who should have access to these weapons. There is no specific need for these in civilian life period.

Erick: You are an intelligent woman and I also think there should be a proper education on guns as well.

The next day I receive another text from his phone with a message.

Erick: Hello Beautiful!

Me: Hello Erick

Erick: I don't know what happened to my WhatsApp

Me: I got a notice that it was no longer a business account that it was now a standard account

Erick: Yeah, beautiful. I don't know what happened to it Mark gave me the phone and I tried texting you but could no longer log in.

Me: It says it is now a standard account. That is weird that it

changed your settings without notification.
Erick: I do not know what Mark did to the phone
Me: Here is some information on the WhatsApp FAQ According to WhatsApp : An "Official business account" does not indicate that WhatsApp endorses this business.

I believe that WhatsApp could not determine that this was a business account and deactivated this account to a standard account. I believe he could no longer access all of his victims together with the other scammers, so he resorted to private phone texts again. WhatsApp accounts can be used by multiple scammers while scamming multiple victims. This is well known in the Romance Scamming business. In fact, most of all of us victims are unaware of this when we sign up on these texting apps.

Erick: I will look at it now, my love
Me: How is your Mother doing?
Erick: She had a little slow challenge but she is a fighter and responding again. Today she had some guest from church. I love you, babe.
Me: That is a blessing she has a good support for healing
Erick: You are a sweet girl and I know you are going to give me family peace. That is the beauty of living especially as we grow older you realize that peace of mind is cheap and most expensive at the same time so when you have it you don't trade it for anything in the world.
Me: Living a most peaceful life it the most important thing you can do for yourself in this lifetime. it is worth more than all the material things in this world. To calm the soul and mind is the most important thing you can do for yourself.
Erick: I am blessed amongst men, I love you. I know I will have you all by my side soon. Honey are you familiar with using Paxful now?
Me: No, what is it?
Erick: It is also an app for bitcoin, my love
Me: I have not heard of it, babe

Erick: Which one did you tell me you are trying out?
Me: I looked into Bitflyer but there is a lot of red tape to set it up. They want your driver license and a lot of personal information.
Erick: Alright beautiful, try Paxful
Me: Ok, my love I will download the app.
Erick: Alright let me know when you do, my love
Me: Babe, I downloaded the app.
Erick: Have you signed up for paxful?
Me: Yes, my love I texted you earlier
Erick: That is great! Did you see how you can link your account to it?
Me: What account?
Erick: Bank account, my love I need you to put your car up for sale because next week I be coming for you.
Me: Ok, I will see what I can do, babe
Erick: My darling you will soon be busy trading or attending meetings and representing me. the boys say they will love to visit Italy before they go back to school.
Me: Oh, are you going to take them?
Erick: Yes, love for a few days. Mom's condition has not allowed us to travel like we usually do. My love, what do you think?

I did not respond because I did not know what to say. It was mid-August, and I had been waiting for three months for him to come and retrieve me. Now he seemed to be able to travel overseas for a few days with the boys. I was totally confused and hurt because I was running low on funds and needed to make a decision soon on whether I was staying or going. I did not plan on staying nor would I have given up my job and home, and now he ws capable of vacationing with his two boys but leaving me hanging. I think this became the turning point of my tolerance of his choices.

Erick: My love, how has your day been?
Me: I am tired and stressed and not sleeping much at all

Erick: You are not happy honey?
Me: Not with the current arrangement, no not happy! This past week has been a nightmare
Erick: What about this past week?
Me: I have been applying for loans and with my current situation it is not being approved.
Erick: Aww, my love you are a reliable arm.
Me: Reliable arm? I am glad you have a sense of humor!
Erick: I love you babe! Do you know why the boys want to go to Italy?
Me: Because they want to and they have a father to provide for them.
Erick: I was there with my late wife when Mark was 7 and Logan was 5. Now they are grown and know what they want so they want us to visit some specific places also for school and social experiences.
Me: When are you leaving?
Erick: I still want to meet up with the Japan ceremony but we leave Tuesday.
Me: This coming Tuesday?
Erick: Yes, my love they go back to school next week
Me: I am glad you are getting some quality time with them before school. I just wish things were different with us.
Erick: They are excited and they made all the bookings.
Me: I hope you have a good trip.
Erick: I am coming to bring you to our house my love as soon as we return.
Me: Good! I will be ready, my love.
Erick: I'm humbled my love and I want to create new memories with you
Me: I hope so my love

The next morning, I received forty photos from him of supposed to be of his Italy trip with the boys. I still cannot understand why he left me hanging after all the promises he had made to me. I gave up a lot and started to feel the repercussions of my decision to move in with him. I think this was the turning point for me that maybe things were not what they seemed, because how can someone who seemed to claim they loved me leave me hanging, especially when he said he is financially capable of supporting me? I asked before about coming to the Vegas or Miami home on my own, and he used the excuse he had a high-tech security system that only he can access. So I cannot enter either homes without him or special codes.

> **Erick:** Thank you, I love you baby you came like an angel in disguise first you were afraid I would hurt you. But how could I hurt an angel like you rather your creator must have reasoned with my late wife who is now one of the creators angels and they chose you as the best woman that will complete me for the remaining of my journey here on earth and also knowing that I am an angel keeper so he entrusted you to my care and also entrusted my heart in your care and all I can say is that since you have accepted me and opened up your heart to me, my world is now complete and my heart is home. I now can't wait to make my covenant of everlasting love at the altar with the priest as my witness and my family and friends witness my oath of love to you as long as I live and then we go on our honeymoon where we will make love like never before and create new beautiful memories together as Mr. and Mrs. Andersen.
> **Me:** I hope all of this comes to pass because I have given all I can give at this point in a relationship. I cannot wait for you to come to me after your return. I love you and miss you my future husband.
> **Erick:** I have no doubt whatsoever of your love my queen.

Another twenty assorted pictures were sent. He seemed to really send massive pictures when he needed to get me to believe everything he is selling. He seemed to be like an overzealous salesman who had a big commission on the line when he completed a sale. I know how far these scammers will go to make you believe their story they are selling. I have several thousand, yes,

Dorothy Harding

THOUSANDS of photos of this man and his family. Most all of us victims believed these scammers based upon the number of photos and the sales campaign they launched. I felt bitter towards the man whose photos were used; in fact, the other victim involved with the scammer also believes the man in the photo is involved in the scam. But I now know he was an innocent victim who may never know the extent of how he was used to scam literally millions out of women. I am one of the few who speak to the other victim in the scam. It is extremely painful to even acknowledge them from our side as a victim also. Did they lose money? No! Did they suffer? Yes, because, for me, it is over but their identity will continue to be used to scam other unsuspecting women. Once they are successful with an identity, they continue to use it over and over with different names and storylines. This is a known fact, because dozens of women have acknowledged being scammed by the same photo of man but with the same or different name and story.

> **Me:** I love the photos they are beautiful, how are the boys?
> **Erick:** They are jetlagged my love but happy. Mom is taking gradual steps my love
> **Me:** That is awesome, babe
> **Erick:** We will be together my love come rain come sunshine this waiting time is the trial time and the time to test our faith that we will be together and we will have a history and story to share among young lovers and it won't be like a fairy tale but a tale.
> **Me:** I will not be looking back at this time fondly in fact you may never hear me discuss it. It has not been a pleasant time for me at all. I was unprepared for the consequences I would have to pay for waiting for you.
> **Erick:** Do you socialize primarily with people from work or with people from the same ethnic/racial/ religious/social economic background? Or do you socialize with a diverse mix of people?
> **Me:** Definitely diverse group of people. I have a few close friends but most people I socialize with are a diverse group of ethnic/religious backgrounds. I have always had a strong

interest of others with different point of views and cultural backgrounds.

Erick: Do you look forward to at least one night out every week or do you prefer to enjoy yourself at home?

Me: As a couple it is good to socialize at least once a week either with another couple or with each other alone. I think it is therapeutic to do date nights regularly.

Erick: I agree with you. Do you enjoy entertaining or do you worry that you will do something wrong or people won't have a good time?

Me: I love to entertain and host parties, babe. I have hosted themed parties and they have all been successful and everyone always had a good time.

Erick: Why am I not surprised, honey

Me: I have hosted baby showers, bridal showers, BBQ's, Wedding Receptions including my own.

Erick: Wow, my multi-talented wife. Is it important for you to attend social events regularly, or does the prospect rarely appeal to you?

Me: I like to attend different social events regularly even though I am a introvert, I like to be around people in a social setting. I love concerts and sporting events too.

Erick: What activities do you enjoy that don't involve your partner?

Me: I enjoy sewing or craft projects but like all activities I can use my significant others input.

Erick: How important is it to you that you and your partner enjoy the same leisure activities?

Me: I think it is important for all couples to enjoy some of the same leisure activities but its more important to learn new and exciting activities that one or the other might be interested in. I think it is healthy to explore these together to learn and grow as one.

Erick: Do you believe that good fences make good neighbors?

Me: I am friendly by nature but I also a private person. I do

> not want to know what my neighbors do privately nor do I want my neighbors to know what I do privately in my home.
> **Erick:** I just want to let you know that I love you, honey
> **Me:** I love you too, babe
> **Erick:** How is everyone?
> **Me:** Alright my love. Did you know they declared a state of emergency in Florida for Hurricane Dorian? Please be safe it is supposed to hit Bahamas too!
> **Erick:** Yeah, my love we have taken precautions.

I am wondering if I had not brought up the Hurricane Dorian, if he would have mentioned it. Because he really was not there but used it as an excuse to put off coming here for me. This weighs on my mind because I gave him the information to use against me.

> **Me:** My love, I missed you
> **Erick:** Did you get my message?
> **Me:** No, I have not received anything from you since last night, Erick
> **Erick:** My love as I take you for my wife, my queen, my soulmate, my best friend I vow to spend my life with you cultivating my love and care for you and all living things. Our relationship is the most important thing to me. It gives me strength. I vow that I put every effort into strengthening it with honesty, patience and faithfulness. For all the days, months and years that we live with each other, I vow to spend every day working to be a truer version of myself. I will make sure that you do the same because I know that together we will reach our desired expectations.
> **Me:** That is beautiful, my love! I love you, babe.
> **Erick:** My love, I leave Bahamas on Saturday
> **Me:** Where are you going?
> **Erick:** But deciding because of the weather
> **Me:** It is a category two now and supposed to be a four by Sunday. They are predicting Sunday Bahamas and Monday Florida.

Erick: Yeah, my love I am moving somethings to Freeport to some properties.
Me: Freeport, Bahamas?
Erick: Yes, my love
Me: I love you and I want you to be safe, babe
Erick: You are my heart
Me: How is everything there? How is your mother doing?
Erick: You know the weather has not been good here.
Me: That is what I was worried about, my love. I pray you and your family stay safe!
Me: Good Morning, I miss and love you.
Erick: My love, I thought I would share my bible scripture this morning, from Ephesians 5, for you were once in darkness but now you are light in the Lord, fruit of the light consists in all goodness, and find out what pleases the lord. Have nothing to do with fruitless deeds of darkness, but rather expose them. It is shameful to mention what the disobedient do in secret, but everything exposed by the light becomes visible, and everything illuminated becomes a light.
Me: My love, is everything ok? I have been worried for you. I have seen some of the devastation there. I love the bible verse by the way.

He sent me an article from the *New York Times*! He was supposed to be there in The Bahamas during a hurricane and had a camera on his phone but no pictures from there! He was supposed to be in Nassau, Bahamas! After all the thousands of pictures he had sent, none had been right at that moment. I never asked him why. I know that The Bahamas has their own TV network. I followed it on Twitter. At times, I started to feel I got more information from social media than from him, and he was there.

Erick: I had some relatives over there who I have sent private rescue team. To assist locate and rescue.
Me: They fear that once this storm pulls away that those who perished will be washed out to sea. I will keep praying for ev-

eryone till this is over.
Erick: Honey is devastating
Me: I know my love, my heart bleeds for everyone there. I am very worried for you and your family.
Erick: I love you, my love. I also lost some personal houses I erected for renting purposes.
Me: I miss you, my love
Erick: I love you my wife and soulmate. What are you doing my darling?
Me: Reading, my love
Erick: I am sure your dividends are waiting for you. Are you reading the same book?
Me: No, I have daily prayers I read at night, babe. Especially with everything going on in our lives now.
Erick: Do you want me to suggest some good reads from my library, then we can review them when we are together?
Me: I would love to hear your suggestions, babe

He sent six photos of someone holding a book; in all photos, they were only of a hand but maybe a child or teenager's hand, and the hand was Caucasian. First was *Leonardo Da Vinci The Biography* by Walter Isaacson; then the second was *The Evolution of Useful Things* by Henry Petroski. Third was *Factualness* by Hans Rosling. Fourth was Carl Sagan's *The Demon Haunted World Science as the Candle in the Dark*. The fifth book was *Reluctant Genius* by Charlotte Gray, and the sixth book was Steven Pinker's *Enlightenment Now: The Case for Reason, Science, Humanism and Progress*. All the photos were taken from the same person at the same time. Could they be Photoshopped? Yes, these scammers have the knowledge and practice on Photoshopping photos, whether they do this themselves or send to another to do. The hand was in different positions and different shadows but seemed to be the same person holding all these books.

Erick: Your mind will never remain the same again, my love. We will get to some levels together.

Me: I will take you up on your suggestions, my love

Erick: I am glad honey and I was really drawn to take some steps back with what has happened in my country and my boys ought to have been back to school, but things are not the same so, I have engaged them in study projects so they both study some books that I will review with them. Also, they are actively involved in their teenage circles to raise aid to those displaced in our dear country Bahamas.

Me: I thought they went back to school before the end of August that's why they wanted the trip to Italy!

Erick: Yeah you know it is even frightening what lies ahead in the future with the burning of the Amazon Forest. These are the days where you have to be a vessel for heaven to reach out and give hope, comfort, direction, healing, shelter, peace to a lot of souls.

Me: Yes, my love

Erick: You are the best thing that has happened to me

Me: I feel the same about you, babe

Erick: I love you and miss you my queen. Well the past few weeks has been hectic but it is gradually getting back to normal.

Me: Glad to hear that, my love

Erick: Deeply appreciate the commitment and dedication we have both said yes to so far in our relationship and the foundation of love we have already built together. It has been a beautiful unfolding of a very beautiful flower. There is no perfection and more of our potential to develop, but I can sense that we are on the verge of something even greater I can sense the purpose in building the love between us to bring more of this love to the world. There is so much to celebrate my wife!

Me: I love and adore you, babe

Erick: What are you doing, my wife?

Me: Adjusting my love. I started a new job and I am working midnights again

Erick: You are back to work, my wife?

Me: Yes, I started a couple weeks ago! I had no choice because I ran out of money!
Erick: I consider myself a blessed man
Me: I tried to apply for a loan and was scammed out of $800 so I must work to recover it.
Erick: You sound like you lost faith
Me: I have faith in god, everyone else has let me down!
Erick: What do you mean everyone else has let you down?
Me: I made some drastic decisions that I may regret now.
Erick: I am sorry you feel that way
Me: How is your family? Are they recovering?
Erick: We are gradually getting back, my love
Me: I pray they do recover, babe
Erick: You know you have a special heart, my love
Me: Thank you, babe
Erick: It will be foolish for me to lose you and I am not a foolish man!
Me: I hope you are not foolish, babe

(He sent a picture of him and his mother again.)

Erick: She is going to be recovering and monitored from home
Me: Wow, that is wonderful, my love. She will be more comfortable at home!
Erick: I told her you needed to see a smile from her.
Me: Yes, I did and good news also
Erick: Do you know there is an opportunity to join me in touching lives of those affected by hurricane in your second country Bahamas.
Me: How can I help, my love. I do not have much to give.
Erick: It doesn't matter how little since your heart is in this. I want to encourage you because even our boys are raising funds and helping families.
Me: How can I assist?

He did not respond to this question, and I did not push. I realize he responded when he wanted to, and I was busy sleeping because I was working nights. I am thankful I had a roof over my head thanks to my brother and was trying to navigate through a recovery of what I have lost.

> **Erick:** My love that reminds me I would love you to sow a seed in the lives of some of the victims in anyway you can.
> **Me:** How can I help? What do they need in shelters? Clothes, shoes or bedding?
> **Erick:** My love I think the funds will be better
> **Me:** I do not have much to give, my love. I am still trying to recover and live until you arrive.
> **Erick:** You can share your donation with bitcoin. I will share wallet of the group I am working with.
> **Me:** What about just donating my dividends from the lithium?
> **Erick:** No, however if you want to buy the group of boys from Mark's league and using bitcoin to raising funds for other kid's needs.
> **Me:** Just send me the wallet ID and I will send him what I can donate
> **Erick:** Alright my wife. I will ask your son Mark to paste it with me so I can share with you. I swear it won't be long anymore. We are coming to the end of our challenge.
> **Me:** This has really been a challenging time
> **Erick:** My love we have a lot of vacations and holidays to go on. I will make up all these months of absence up to you I swear! And you know what the reward is for patience right!
> **Me:** Yes, my love
> **Erick:** Do you want me to get the wallet from Mark now?
> **Me:** Whatever is convenient for him. I won't get paid for a few days.
> **Erick:** Are they paying you what your efforts are worth now?

Me: Better than most make but only half of what I used to make before.
Erick: It is not going to be for long, my wife. I swear to you!
Me: I hope not much longer it has been too long already, Erick
Erick: My love are you making a list?
Me: List of what?
Erick: Things you want us to do together to bring you joy!
Me: I will have to think on it, babe
Erick: Romans 8:28 And we know that God causes all things to work together for good to those who love God, to those who are called according to his purpose.
Me: Love is patient, Love is kind. It does not envy, it does not boast, it is not proud. It does not dishonor others, it is not self seeking, it is not easily angered, it keeps no record of wrongs. 1 Corinthians 13:4-5
Erick: I love you Mrs. Donna Andersen
Me: I love you, too Erick I purchased some bitcoin I can only afford $100 and that is more than I can spare.
Erick: You are an amazing woman, my love. I will like you to add more to that my love I have a reason, my queen!

I never responded because it was too much for me to afford already. I gave up everything and had received nothing in return but broken promises, and it started to get to me. I struggled financially and emotionally with this situation I put myself in. I totally regret making the rash decision to give up my personal belongings and life for this man I hadn't even met yet. I was embarrassed and kept to myself all the time, and I am not a depression-type person, but I now know I sank into a bad state of mind. I did not feel joy in this relationship, and I needed to know what was going on with this person I was corresponding with. I tried on several occasions to Google his name and do a background check, but nothing ever came up. I figured maybe because he was from The Bahamas, outside the United States, that is why! His Facebook page was sparse at the least, so I could not verify anything on him, so I took him at his word, but I was drained from the emotional roller coaster he put me on. By now, it was the middle of October 2019.

Erick: How is the seed fund to the hurricane victims, my love
Me: It has gained quite a bit more than I expected it is at $150 and the hold will be lifted tomorrow.
Erick: Alright my love. I will inform Mark about that.
Me: I wish it was more but this is more than I can afford.
Erick: Yeah, my love is the window you know it is going to skyrocket and other coins are rotating. you now know it is when bitcoin has more value. When bitcoin is low the more the value.
Me: You are the financial expert and I am still learning, babe
Erick: You impress me a lot my wife. I cannot tell you how proud I am of you. Me and other parents are assisting the school to erect it back to some temporary classrooms to accommodate students in the affected classes so today I had to be taken through all the progress and video presentation and had to raise some funds today which I did not plan for.
Me: Well, I think it is important for the kids to have a place to learn.
Erick: Honey those other kids that have parents that are struggling need shoulders to lean on as well
Me: Yes, I am sure they do
Erick: My love, you are not happy today?
Me: No, I am not happy at all
Erick: I know but what is the main reason, my love?
Me: It does not matter because I have suffered the consequences of my own actions and I struggle daily as a result.
Erick: What do you mean?
Me: I have to rebuild I have given up to be with you and I am struggling and I should not have had to so, no I am not happy!
Erick: My love, I want to assure you that I will make it up to you. I hope that your life with me is so wonderful that when you are awake, you wonder if you are dreaming and when

your dreaming you wonder if you are awake.

He sent me an article by bitcoinist.com. The article was "Bitcoin (BTC) Supply Could Be Blown Above 21M." This seemed to be a legitimate article. I started to question everything he sent me at this point.

Erick: I would like you to read this article, my wife
Me: I will when I get a chance
Erick: My queen you are my might. You know even banks are trying to move into the bitcoin industry. I will love your lips to be the first I kiss every morning when I wake and the last I kiss before I go to bed every night. I want your ear to be the most I tell the words I love you!
Me: That is sweet, babe
Erick: My love, what platform do you want to share your bitcoin? or Paxful?
Me: Coinbase, babe
Erick: Ok, my love here is my wallet ID
Me: I am sending $189.57 now
Erick: Ok love you can share $150 and when you add to it you can share the rest.
Me: I have bills and car insurance to pay right now I have no extra to spare to donate!
Erick: Yeah I know my love. How much more are you thinking to reinvest wife of mine? I want to plan to guide you.
Me: I do not know how much more I can invest! I have to support myself fully right now because I have no idea when you are coming. I sent the $150 bitcoin to the wallet ID you sent tell Mark that is all I can afford to donate.
Erick: Everything is going to be alright I promise OK?
Me: I hope so, Erick because I am tapped out financially and emotionally too.
Erick: You are more precious than the most precious gem. You are sweeter than sugar. You are more enchanting than moonlight. You are special, exquisite, unique and delightful,

all at once. And the best thing is, somehow you chose me to be with you. I love you, Donna!
Me: I miss you, babe
Erick: Did I wake you?
Me: No, I am working tonight
Erick: My sincere apologies for the late response, my wife
Me: I hope everything is ok there babe
Erick: A close associate of mine lost his dad today and when he told me I felt really sad for him.
Me: That is sad, babe
Erick: Well that is a sad feeling but can be a celebration of life when the person lives to the ripe old age.
Me: That is good but not everyone especially the family looks at it as a celebration too. Keep that in mind babe.
Erick: That is true, my love
Me: I love you too. My love
Erick: Not really I am some parents had to put up a tutorial center for the remainder of the term in A private center while supporting the school to restructure.
Me: What?
Erick: So it has been a very busy week my love
Me: Is this referring to the boys education or the children displaced there?
Erick: Education my love
Me: Is the tutorial center for all the children?
Erick: Not all my love only those that can access for now.

Most of our conversations were like this where he would make a statement and not explain himself or what he was referring to in the conversation. Sometimes I wondered if he was talking to me or responding to another person. A lot of things were never really explained, like this conversation. These are real conversations between me and him or others.

Me: Are the boys assisting you?

Dorothy Harding

(No response to my question! Avoidance was becoming the normal response now. No excuses, no nothing!)

Erick: I just want you to know that you can behold little time and I will be with you.
Me: I have to keep working so I may be able to retire within the next 7 years.
Erick: I think you don't have to work your ass that long with me.
Me: I hope not or I should not be with you at all!
Erick: Alright my wife that is smart thinking. The house of mine is almost complete.
Me: That is good because the sooner it is, the sooner we can be together, babe.
Erick: What we have together is unique. It is a special bond that is strong and unbreakable. We can make it through anything we encounter and we only grow stronger from the trials we face together. Together we are strong. Being with you has made me a better person and I can't believe that I found you. Ever since I met you, I never want to let you go. The attraction that you and I share is one that is so intense and I never want to be separated from you. How is your passport Honey?
Me: My passport is good I just renewed it remember?
Erick: Yes, I remember and I am proud of you! Mom said she wants to be ready for to cook Christmas meal with you and was already inviting her friends and she says she would love to make a cake like the angel statue, if you can assist, my love.
Me: Nothing would make me happier, babe.
Erick: Alright Mrs. Andersen because today I was taking her to visit her friends, she said she would love to return to the states with me to welcome you.
Me: Then you grant her whatever wishes she wants
Erick: I love you babe and miss you. One of my senior staff lost his son yesterday
Me: I miss you too and what happened to senior staff?

Erick: The son passed away my love
Me: OMG, that is terrible, my love what happened?
Erick: Was involved in an accident.
Me: That is awful, babe
Erick: Honey, I need your PayPal details
Me: Why?
Erick: You can use it to buy bitcoin like you did before, OK
Me: You cannot use PayPal to buy bitcoin not through Coinbase they require bank account or credit card.
Erick: I will walk you through it and show you how.

Prior to this conversation, I had used PayPal for my personal use only. He called me and asked to use PayPal to accept payments from his office manager, Ann Daniels. She sent me fifty dollars through my PayPal account. Later, another smaller transaction came through; then PayPal shut down my account. He attempted to pass a large amount, one thousand dollars, to me, and PayPal put all funds in my account on hold indefinitely.

Erick: My love, This was a trial to add you as a recipient Ok?
Me: Ok, but why not you buy the bitcoin yourself if it is coming from your business manager? Why am I having to receive funds to purchase bitcoin from your business?
Erick: Hold on first my love ok until the full amount is sent ok?
Me: What are you talking about full amount, my PayPal is a personal account not a business account. I cannot use it to receive large amount of funds with no questions asked! I hope you understand!
Erick: What are you doing? My love you have me and the Andersen's as well to look after you and I need you to take care of this for me.
Me: I have a memorial service for my Aunt to attend we will discuss this later!
Erick: I will make it all up to you and I am sorry for your loss.

Me: We will talk later!

Erick: How are you my love? I have not heard from you since we talked. Is everything ok with your PayPal? Because after we told you said you had to call PayPal that you tried to receive more fund but it is not coming through!

Me: I was sleeping all day I had to work. It said it shut it down because she tried to withdraw $4950 from my account and I do not have that kind of money in my account.

At this point I did not understand what was happening, only that his office manager, Ann, was attempting to withdraw funds from my account, and PayPal shut it down. I now realize he was pulling the strings and trying to access funds from me through my PayPal account, and then he could pad his account. I did not realize he was using me to move money for him through my PayPal account. This did not happen. Due to issues, PayPal shut it down, and I grew extremely suspicious of his intention. It is my understanding that this money was returned because eventually PayPal lifted the hold, and the money was returned to where it came from. I refused any further access to accept any further money from him or anyone associated with him. I later realized Ann Daniels was not his office assistant but another victim he was scamming. The money was hers, not his business account money. The money was not sent back to her after PayPal. Do I know where it went? Probably to him. It was not my money nor did I keep any of it. At the time, neither me nor Ann knew that this man was not who he said he was!

Erick: That was an error okay from my assistant!

I never responded. I was furious that this transaction between us occurred and did not feel proper. I had seriously questioned this relationship and if we would actually end up together.

Erick: My love, Ann is having challenges with PayPal and would have to deposit the money into another account so can you give me your banking details ok!

Me: My bank has heavy security on my account after I was

scammed they heavily monitor all my transactions now. I do not want to divulge any of my banking details to anyone at the time! I am sorry she cannot use PayPal!
Erick: I gave Ann your email did you get an apology?
Me: Apology? For what?
Erick: For the mistake of requesting money from you
Me: I figured it was a mistake and she cancelled it immediately. I notified you and she corrected it no problem.

It was now the end of November, and I was consumed with anxiety over all his broken promises and realizing he would not be coming and deciding what I need to do. I was recovering but regretted investing any money because I never received any further dividends as promised. Not one promise had been met, and I was very angry with him and growing distant. I did not talk to anyone about what was going on and was feeling extremely embarrassed over my decisions to believe his story!

Erick: My love, your unconditional love has healed my wounds and brought me back to a place I thought I could never be. Happy Thanksgiving, my love and may I never cease to be thankful for you.
Me: That is sweet but it is past Thanksgiving now but I understand that where you are Thanksgiving is not celebrated.
Erick: The first time I heard you say the words, "I love you," it was like I had been to Cloud 9. because it came from a genuine heart, and I have not come down until now. Right after you uttered those words, I asked myself "Do I have all it takes to love her the best way she deserves?" As I looked for an answer, I asked again: "Have she given me any reason not to? "No, just more reasons to love her more and more. I then realized that I had already fallen in love with you, and I am so in love with you still. In the past after my late wife passed away, I had always yearned for someone to love, to cherish, and to take good care of and someone with whom I could share my dreams and who help me make them come

true. I had always walked around feeling an emptiness that I thought would never get filled, but since I met you, the genuineness of your love has filled that hole. I think back to how empty my life was without you, and I am so grateful that you are here now. I have found in you what it means to love. I tell you a hundred times a day, everyday that I love you. Although you return these feelings and love me too. I do not know if you understand the magnitude of what they mean to me. You may not realize it, but when you do the slightest thing for me, it warms my heart. Each day I fall more in love with you.
Me: I wish you were here to tell me this to my face but I know realistically that it is not happening. I hope all is well with you and your family.
Erick: Yes, we will be together soon, my love Are you ready to share this Christmas with me?
Me: I would love nothing more than to spend Christmas with you!
Erick: I promise you that! I want you to buy more bitcoin for investment even taking out a loan.
Me: I hope this promise comes true. I cannot take out a loan because I was scammed it is impossible right now to get a loan.
Erick: You are my match made in heaven. There is never a second where you aren't there to lift me up when I need you to. I am so fortunate to have crossed paths with you in the beginning. it has brought us to this beautiful point in our lives. You are everything I could have wanted in a woman. I will never want anything or anyone else. That I can promise.
Me: That is very sweet you feel this way but the true test is when we are finally together until then it is all relevant.
Erick: My love, any luck on a loan?
Me: No, babe no luck, sorry

It started to wear on me, his insisting on me to obtain a loan for any amount and me trying to recover from the loss of income, because I invested thousands into Bitcoin for lithium investment. When we did talk on the phone, it was me explaining constantly why I have no money. In my head I knew this was not a normal relationship and chances were slim we would ever meet. But I had no proof who he was or who he wasn't.

> **Erick:** I want to bring everyone to Miami
> **Me:** For Christmas?
> **Erick:** Yeah honey
> **Me:** Including me?

No response, of course, and the cat and mouse game started to wear on me. I knew chances of seeing him for Christmas weren't happening; it became an awful sinking feeling in my gut. I was excited to hear from him but, at the same time, dreaded the disappointment he was bringing. I was sinking into a depressive state and needed to make a decision soon.

> **Erick:** I am feeling really let down by your reasons to invest any further money in lithium. You say you love me but are no longer fighting for us and looking out for our future together.
> **Me:** I have to put a roof over my own head and pay my own bills because I cannot count on you or your excuses. I am sorry but this is how I feel!
> **Erick:** Thank you for your sincerity because I will repay your love and patience with my faithfulness as long as I live this is my promise.
> **Me:** I hope so, Mr. Andersen
> **Erick:** The boys are with me now and Mom is really fighting to make sure she is ready for Christmas.
> **Me:** Don't let her overdo it, babe. I will help her whenever I arrive.
> **Erick:** My love I got a call from my manager there are some changes in the office so never respond to any email from Ann if you can block the email we are making some changes.
> **Me:** Ok, my love

This was December 20, 2019, and five days before Christmas and no mention of coming to get me. This date is relevant because it dotted some lines and crossed some t's in the end.

>**Erick:** My love, Mom asked after her angel today.
>**Me:** The angel is waiting for her son to come and retrieve us!
>**Erick:** It is going to be a triumphant entry, my love
>**Me:** I cannot wait!
>**Erick:** My love is everything OK?
>**Me:** Yes, for now Erick
>**Erick:** Did you see my vow letter to you?
>**Me:** Yes, I did not know if you had time for me to respond
>**Erick:** What do you mean love? I don't understand and feel a bit disappointed. I took the time to write you that letter and you read and said nothing. Does it mean the letter meant nothing to you?
>**Me:** I love the letter it was beautiful, my love
>**Erick:** But you went quiet all along! You don't know how much I love your response of assurance.
>**Me:** I am sorry I did not know that you needed assurance from a love letter, my love
>**Erick:** But you are the only woman I commit and communicate with
>**Me:** I am sorry, my love. I wait to hear daily and eager to see you appear and am disappointed it is taking so long but you are always on my mind.
>**Erick:** You know that I will reward you for your loyalty and commitment.
>**Me:** I was waiting to hear from you if we were to be together for Christmas, my love
>**Me:** My love?

(No answer???)

>**Me:** I love you and have the ability of forgiveness but I re-

quire the truth at all times. You seem upset with me for not responding to your commitment letter yesterday but you do not respond to my questions. I have given up everything to be with you and expect truthful answers. You said we would be together for Christmas and never said no more. You said that you loved me in gods name but cannot make a commitment. Am I expecting too much to ask for you to follow through on your promises and commitment to me? I have more than proved my commitment to you and expect the same in return. I have sacrificed enough to and complied to your wishes and deserve the same in return.

Erick: My love, thank you so much for this sincere letter and I want to speak with you over the phone. When can I call you?

Me: I am available anytime.

He called, and I could barely hear him; it seemed it was not actually connecting properly.

Erick: Could you hear me, my love

Me: No, babe it was all in and out the connection was bad

Erick: The connection is bad here in Nassau

Me: Good Morning, Mr. Andersen

Erick: Are you angry with me

Me: No, you just need to work on your communication skills

Erick: My honest apologies and you know the boys are extra work. That is why I cannot wait to begin life with you this year is one of my most challenging. I never expected it to be this way in my love. I promise you that I will not let you down. I swear on the grave of my last wife! I am even affected with my work but Mom wants to fight. So, I am getting a doctor to operate on her but they want me to bring her to India.

Me: What? Why India? What operation does she need?

Erick: Yeah, her backbone needs fluid my love. It is very painful to her.

Me: Disc or synovial fluid? What about injections? They can inject cortisone into her lower back to ease the pain.

Erick: My love it had been done before but I think her age is affecting the effect that is why I am flying her to India and she really wants to bond with you. She really wants to meet the woman who will be the new woman in our life.

By now it was two days prior to Christmas and another broken promise. I noticed prior to every date he promised to come for me, Mom's health deteriorated. I knew in my gut he was not coming, and I was very upset; plus, who goes to India for back surgery when you are right next to United States? I was baffled by his decision and could not make sense of it. But knew he was never coming to get me. But he had to find a way to continue to string me along for the scam.

Me: I do not understand your decision at this time! I would reconsider this surgery and how will she make it to India in her current condition if she cannot make it here to United States!

Erick: I wanted to tell you today how good I feel about us and about us and about our future together. I enjoy the thoughts of the future with you It seems that everything we do is even more meaningful because it isn't just for today—it is for always. You make me feel truly happy, and I'll always love making you feel special.

Me: I am sorry but I am having a hard time right now this decision you made has caused me grief.

Erick: I'm sorry I will make it up to you everyday of my living.

Me: It is just another day without you! I did not celebrate Christmas this year. I am depressed now.

Erick: On this Christmas season I have so many things I would like to tell you. The first one is that I am really happy to be a part of your life. I feel blessed because I am in love with such a good woman like you are and that fact that you feel the same way as me. You have changed my life completely since you have been by my side and I am really happy each day of the week. So on this Christmas I wish many things for you: My love on this Christmas I wish you to enjoy a beautiful day with your whole family, I wish the little child Jesus to be in your heart and the blessings to fill your home. I really wish you to keep that inner peace and happiness each day of your entire life. I hope God to be present on every act you do in your life.

Me: Merry Christmas! I hope you had a wonderful day.

Erick: No, my love. Mom was unconscious all throughout and just regained her consciousness.

Me: Why? My love

Erick: My divine wife I love you so much

Me: How is Mom?

Erick: My love I got her favorite jazz artist here to play her favorite songs all night now that she is awake like a new person but I am still making plans to fly her so that she can be ready for our lives next year. I miss you!

Me: I hope it all works out for you and her and she gets the treatment she requires. Just keep me updated, Erick

Erick: I consider myself everyday blessed to know that I have the most amazing woman patiently waiting for me and standing by my side, my love.

Me: I hope you feel that way but I feel I am not truly by your side I am a million miles away and soon to be further. This has put more strain on the relationship even further but you have to do what you think is best and so do I.

Erick: You are a very strong woman and I know when we are finally together I will do my best to take care of you. I promise you that OK! I am going to get my father-in-law shortly.

Me: I forgot your in-laws are also there. Are the boys spending some quality time with them also?

Erick: I love you my queen. I am looking forward to have an office for you by my side and I know we will do wonders.

Me: I hope it all works out for us.

Erick: Yes, my love we are entering into a new decade

Me: I hope 2020 is a better year for us then 2019 has been.

Erick: How are you doing my love? Tell me?

Me: I have spent the day mostly in prayer and solitude, Erick.

Erick: That is how it should be. Have you made any list?

Me: List of what?

Erick: Of things we have to achieve together for the new year. I had a dream last night.

Me: I pray for health and happiness and for us to finally be together.

Erick: I know my love but you don't feel the energy! Are you getting weak, my love?

Me: Weak? If I was weak I would of ditched you several months ago but I am looking for brighter days ahead whether you are a part of them or not. I have had my dreams shattered so many times this past year but I need something good to outweigh the bad that has happened.

Erick: My love when we are together our story will inspire young lovers.

Me: I listened to a sermon this morning. He said god puts those in your life for a reason. If someone was meant to be in your life they will remain, if they are not they will leave. It is all God's will.

Erick: You know our relationship is like when you sow a seed. You know the seed has to take root Then begin to grow and bring branches and fruits.

Me: But a seed has to be nurtured and protected to thrive not planted and left to thrive on its own because chances are it will become diseased and die.

Erick: It is taking roots and the deeper the roots the greater the tree. That is how our love is.

Me: Ok

Erick: I am sorry, my love. It is coming to an end I assure you of that OK

Scammed in America

> **Me:** Just keep in touch is all I ask
> **Erick:** Happy New Year, my wife
> **Me:** Happy New Year, Erick
> **Erick:** We leave for India on Saturday, Jan. 4th OK
> **Me:** I hope it all works out for you.

It was several days before I heard any more from Erick, and it was very sporadic when I finally did. He never went into details of what exactly this surgery was to entail or why India. Communication had been waning between us, and I was growing further distant and losing interest in this relationship. He did start noticing something was happening, but I think he was scared I would sever all ties between us at this point.

> **Erick:** Thank you for your patience and I will never let you down.
> **Me:** I hope not but I feel that is already happened
> **Erick:** But destiny is keeping you for us. Mom is getting prepped for surgery
> **Me:** I pray for a good outcome and a swift recovery
> **Erick:** Thank you, my love. But it has not been a really good day. I lost my purse and still hoping to recover it as well.
> **Me:** That is awful I hope you recover it
> **Erick:** We need a holiday to get away. A pamper season
> **Me:** I will look forward to that when it happens
> **Erick:** And I promise us that OK
> **Me:** How is your mother's surgery?
> **Erick:** My wife her surgery was very successful
> **Me:** Thank God! I have been worried for her.
> **Erick:** Oh, my love you know I need to teach you how to trade so you can be trading and make better money while I am still treating Mom then when we are together I will show you other ways.
> **Me:** I am willing to learn from you, Mr. Andersen
> **Erick:** I will love you to buy shares my love this month and be a pioneer investor or shareholder then I will make you my

trustee so that you can be signatory to all the factories that will be set-up in Bahamas and the states to be a pioneer is a great advantage, my queen.

Me: I love you, babe

Erick: My love, how are you doing?

Me: Exhausted my love but hanging in there

Erick: Did you work today?

Me: Yes, I work a lot babe

Erick: We will be coming back by grace this weekend, my love

Me: Back to the Bahamas? How is your Mom?

Erick: Yes, love and she is getting back gradually

Me: She is fighting for you and the boys and she has a strong will to live

Erick: She loves you as well she is determined to meet you because she knows you have my heart.

Me: When we finally get together I would like her to stay with us as she heals to regain her strength.

Erick: I love you

Erick: Do you know bitcoin increased with some dividends?

Me: No, my love

Erick: Check your wallets love. The excitement I get when I think of our lives together is amazingly exciting.

Me: I am excited for our future together, too

Erick: You are my completeness when I set out to find you I just knew you were going to be an angel. My love did you check your wallets?

Me: Yes, it says bitcoin is up 1.21%

Erick: Yes, and even more yesterday. How much do you have in your wallets?

Me: I am hoping to be able to buy more soon but I gave you everything I had in my wallet. The last I bought was $40 and I transferred it to you to give to Mark for donation. **Erick:** Alright my love. Dividends are coming this year I am excited. Did you remember the silicon I discussed with you?

Scammed in America

Me: Yes, and is that purchased with bitcoin also?

Erick: Yes, my love and you know its like buying first tokens like some of us that bought the bitcoin first token. We know how much it is work now.

Me: I will see what I can do this month. When my car broke down it wiped out any extra I had and I am playing catch up on my bills ever since. I live on a very strict budget and it takes me a while to save up any extra money.

Erick: Well one thing I know for certain is that our creator cannot give us a path to walk through filled only with stormy weather. No, just like every seed planted to the soil, we need rain and sun to get deeper roots and spring forth with fruits of experiences that we can pass along to our generations. My love as soon as we are back I am coming for you.

Me: I love you and cannot wait to see you babe

Erick: Mom needs to stay some days to get approval to travel with medication

Me: I hope she feels better soon

Erick: Are you aware of the coronavirus?

Me: Yes, I am worried for you and your mother. Please be careful and take all precautions

Erick: My love how come you are this sweet?

Me: Thank you but I am growing wary at this point. It has been over 10 months and we have been plagued with bad luck and no light at the end of tunnel. And now a possible pandemic!

Erick: My love I promise we will not let you down as a family. We have to fly mom to Abu Dhabi because of the coronavirus to wait for her medication before she can return because of her age she has been delicate.

Me: Please be careful they already have several cases here in the states already. Keep me posted my love.

Erick: I will need you to get busy with our plans because there are chances you will come meet us In Abu Dhabi.

Me: I have a feeling things will get worse before it gets better

Erick: I love you! My love the boys need some things you will have to assist me with. I need to get the boys some cards.
Me: What do they need?
Erick: You know that gift card? Something like a visa gift card like this one. He sent me a photo of a visa gift card.
Me: But these gift cards are only good in the US, my love Where are the boys? I thought they were in the Bahamas!
Erick: They are in Miami and they need resources from me

I was really confused because he had an office with staff in Miami, Vegas, and New York with a brother here in New York. Why did I need to provide anything for them? He claimed to have property and money. I was struggling to keep afloat and recover from the long wait for him to come get me so we could be together. I had felt like I slipped down a rabbit hole and was digging my way to the surface again. It was late January, and no relief in sight.

Me: Ok, how much do they need and when?
Erick: They need up to a thousand my love but I don't know how much you can afford my love and when
Me: I cannot access a thousand dollars. I simply do not have that kind of money right now maybe a hundred or two.
Erick: Alright my wife. How much can you send?
Me: Maybe $150 - $200 at the most
Erick: I know you can do more if you had the ability. So many unforeseen circumstances and we will in Dubai this Wednesday, my love.
Me: How is Mom doing, babe?
Erick: She is still being observed in the vented ward, my love
Me: My prayers are with her, my love
Erick: She has regained consciousness
Me: That's good, what is the prognosis?
Erick: How are you? I know you are super mad with me.
Me: I am worried about you and your decisions and us. Erick
Erick: I promise that I will come get you as soon as mom is back with me in the Bahamas and strong. I am also thinking

you should come here if possible.
Me: I do miss you but I would feel better coming to you in Bahamas versus overseas.
Erick: Thank you for understanding
Me: I miss you, babe
Erick: My love your boys need that card, today
Me: I would love to but I do not have the money! My car insurance went up and I need every dime I make to survive. I am so sorry but I cannot help them out at this time.
Erick: My queen you changed!
Me: I changed? I gave up a lot to be with you and you put us on hold. I need to support myself and have invested a lot of money with no return with you and for our future. You have not contributed to my finances or well being. I am on my own with no help and now you want me to help you and send money to your boys? I need to concentrate on my needs and I am sorry for the predicament you are in. I pray for you and your family.

I received no response from him. It seemed when I claimed to be in need, he grew cold and did not comment. But I was to jump at every chance to help and support him financially. I was considering ending this relationship because I saw no end to the excuses of why he could not come here anymore. I didn't hear about his brother's involvement in his mother's care. I had slowly pulled back my affections and needed to think of myself now.

Erick: My queen how are you? What are you doing?
Me: Going through personal paperwork for insurance.
Erick: Can you use bitcoin to get the card?
Me: You cannot us bitcoin to buy gift cards in store I do not know about online.
Erick: There is a website I will send you that you can use to buy gift cards with bitcoin
Me: egifter.com?
Erick: I can add to that when I am settled. Can you buy for Mark he needs the cards for an Assignment and they cannot

access anything till I am back in Bahamas.

Me: I need money to buy bitcoin or you can send me some bitcoin.

Erick: You can buy at gift card mall or Walmart gift card.

Me: You cannot buy Walmart gift cards with bitcoin.

Erick: Which one can you buy?

Me: Just regular visa gift card with bitcoin.

Erick: You can convert bitcoin to cash then use that to buy Walmart gift cards

Me: I do not know how to do that, Erick!

Erick: I will walk you through it, my love

Me: I will need the cash before I can buy the Walmart gift card

Erick: My love, do you think you can change that Walmart it is the wrong one.

Me: That is the only Walmart gift card and once I purchase it is not refundable, Erick!

Erick: My wife, he said he can't use it that it is not the Visa card or MasterCard that is accepted. I will share $100 with you to buy two for him $50 and $50 ok?

Me: I cannot buy Visa or MasterCard gift cards with bitcoin. I have to physically buy them with cash and I do not have the cash to pay for it!

Erick: Oh, my love if I send you bitcoin do you know how to sell it?

Me: No, you have not showed me how to sell bitcoin for cash!

Erick: I will teach you everything because I am confident in you.

Me: I hope so after all this mess you have me deal with.

Erick: Please never again bring in murmuring and complaints about the past in this relationship. let your heart give the best to this relationship so that when we are together you will enjoy all the reward of patience because I will never let you down.

> **Me:** I hope you never let me down because it will end this relationship quickly.
> **Erick:** I trust you and I trust our creator and I know for certain that he has destined us to be together.
> **Me:** I hope so, my love or we are doomed to fail
> **Erick:** Mom is getting ready to fly back I have placed an order for her robotic chair
> **Me:** Please be careful traveling this coronavirus is getting worse from what I am hearing.
> **Erick:** Do you still have the info on those cards you bought for Mark?

He called me and walked me through the process of selling Bitcoin for cash, then depositing it into my bank account. He sent me $125 in Bitcoin and with fees to convert to cash; it was just a few dollars over one hundred. I then purchased two Walmart gift cards online for fifty dollars each and sent him the card info electronically as a e-card. He then stated that Mark did not want that kind, but there was no refund or exchange on e-cards.

> **Me:** The Walmart cards were the last ones sent and that was sent directly to you.
> **Erick:** That is correct but can you resend it?
> **Me:** When purchased Walmart sent the e-card directly to you that info never came from me.
> **Erick:** Which one did you send to this number?
> **Me:** Walmart for $50 to erickandersen44@gmail.com
> **Erick:** Alright we have to get a American Express for Mark. He said they were advised to try Amex.
> **Me:** I do not know how to get a American Express Gift Card. I have never seen them as gift cards in the stores.
> **Erick:** Ok, but try to find out my love. Or maybe a MasterCard if not.
> **Me:** You need to send me some money to buy gift cards, I do not have any extra money.

Dorothy Harding

On February 23, 2020, my sister texted me a message: "Hey, not sure if you still have a relationship with Erick Andersen because the last time we talked you were, but while I was running a name for identity checks for work I ended up on a website called ScamHaters United Ltd. While I was on there I seen Erick's name on there too. Here is the site." I clicked the link she sent me, and my heart dropped in my stomach. There was Erick's name and face listed as a fake identity with another innocent man's face. I was in shock and sick to my stomach. Who was this man whom I have been corresponding with for a year? This seemed to be a legitimate site, but I needed more info. It seemed, in my investigation, that Erick Andersen did not exist. Do I know who the man I spoke to and messaged daily was? No, I didn't. I did check on the man whose pictures were sent in the thousands to me stating to be Erick Andersen, and they belonged to a businessman in California. I ran a background check, and this man was legitimately an American businessman who was of Latino decent, not Bahamian! When Erick and I originally met and talked, the man whose photos were used was on vacation in Mexico with his beautiful wife and family. His mother was deceased also! The more I learned, the more angry I became. I wanted to know who this man was and what his motive was for me. Apparently, Ann the office assistant who worked for Erick and whom he let go in December was the one who reported him to ScamHaters United Ltd. This group is legit, and they work as a non-profit around the world educating victims of Romance Scams. This organization works to uncover who is behind these scams. I continued to speak with Erick until I had enough proof that he was not who he claimed to be. I had to come to terms with the fact that I was catfished by some strange man or group from around the world. I was in so much pain because I believed I was in a relationship with a man and invested my hard-earned money into lithium for our future. I now know I will never see a penny of my money back, and I needed to end this scam quickly and painlessly as possible. This was how it ended!

Erick: I miss you here is a video I made for you, my love.

The video consisted of a series of photos of the man whose identity he stole to scam me and who knows how many other women out of thousands of dollars.

> **Me:** What is The Camp?
> **Erick:** No love was making you a video Champ?
> **Me:** It is on your shirt and pants? I knew what it meant I wanted him to come clean and tell the truth but did not expect it at this point.
> **Erick:** Yes, is a gift from my boys
> **Me:** Really?
> **Erick:** Yes, love are you surprised? You don't seem to like it!

He was scared I found out the truth to his identity. I could tell by his messages.

> **Me:** That's funny because when I googled it this came up???

I sent him a link to the identity of the real man in the pictures he had been using on me for a year!

> **Erick:** It was the company I ran with my late wife that my ex ruined with my procurement manager …they used my credentials to run it
> **Erick:** You reminding me of tormenting pain
> **Erick:** I shouldn't have sent the video!
> **Me:** Then who is this legitimate man or who is Erick Andersen?
> **Erick:** You know already
> **Erick:** My identity was coming and I am in court process
> **Erick:** I told you when we began
> **Me:** You lied to me for a year! When I asked what The Camp meant you could not come clean! you think I am some stupid woman and would never find out you are not whom you portray to be. The truth always comes out!

I never heard from Erick Andersen again! I was raw with anger over how this happened to me, an intelligent, hardworking woman! I was distraught with rage! Who was this man, and why me? I wanted to find out more. I inquired with Ann Daniels, his ex-office manager whom I still had her email address to. She was glad I contacted her. She met Erick Andersen on Zoosk also! Probably after I did! She was curious, and her niece ran a check on him and found out he was not who he said he was; she knew the true identity of the man in the photos Erick was using, and it all come to a close in late December 2019. This was the same time he asked me to not have any contact with her or receive emails from her. I was sickened that I was not his only victim! Why had I not seen any signs? I was on a quest to educate myself on all things romance scam because this is what it is called. Some refer to it as catfished, but when there is money involved, it became Romance Scam. I am forever grateful to Scam-Haters United Ltd. They are a wealth of information on all things related to romance scamming and all issues related. They stay up on the latest information and quickly inform you of what to be on the lookout for. Initially, I Googled romance scams, and a link to an investigation by a Canadian news network came up. It described a woman who was scammed out of two million dollars. She sold her life to these scammers. Apparently, there are groups of scammers who work on their victims in unison to drain every last penny out of an unsuspecting woman. She gave everything she worked for, her property, prized artwork, wiped out bank accounts, retirement. They then convinced her that she was in legal trouble and the authorities were after her. That was the last straw, and she drove to a secure place and blew her own brains out! I cried after reading her story. I knew then I had to speak up about my own story and report what happened to me to authorities. I will not recover any of my money back, that I know. Anyone who claims to be able to recover your money is running a scam on you. Because the income leaves the country of your origin immediately; you cannot track it. Some can trace it, but only if they discover the identity of the scammer. These scammers are sometimes known as Yahoo Boys. They lurk on Facebook, Instagram, and all dating websites. They prey on lonely, unsuspecting middle-aged women. Widows, divorced, and sometimes married women are their targets. Like my story, they lure you into a relationship and then make promises they cannot keep. They then ask for money due to an emergency issue, and the unsuspecting victim has no clue what is really going on. I have joined support groups and have talked to dozens of other victims who gave all of their life savings to these scammers. My loss is minimal compared to those I spoke to. I can financially recover; most do not. I was sick to my stomach at the heartbreak and suffering these women endured.

This scam spans the globe. It is in Canada, Australia, UK, Germany, Sweden, The Philippines, Mexico, and throughout the world. ScamWatcher is based in Australia. There is an organization, Advocating Against Romance Scammers, here in United States. They are a non-profit organization providing awareness and advocacy for those affected by online romance scams. One of the co-founders is a victim of the online romance scam. He had his identity stolen to scam literally thousands of women. He found his likeness used on fifteen sites and counting. He still receives contact from women who were scammed using his pictures. He can only take down and remove sites he finds, but they continue to reappear elsewhere. That is why he continues to work hard to prevent and stop these scammers. There are two victims to these scams: "the client," as we are referred as by scammers, and the men and women whose pictures were stolen from social media.

I literally paid a dating website to fix me up with a scammer. There is currently no legislature on the books protecting innocent women from these scammers. Social media is full of hundreds of thousands of scammers waiting and lurking for their victims, both male and female. If you receive a friend request on Facebook and you do not know this person, chances are they are a scammer. I have received lots of followers on Instagram from strange men who want to talk. I block and delete them. I set my Facebook to private, but they can seep in through a friend's account. These scammers are sophisticated; they can hack banks, emails, Facebook and Instagram accounts. I cannot stress how important it is as a middle-aged woman to be aware of what is going on and educate yourself. Some women are scammed multiple times; this is not uncommon. I have chosen to fight and advocate against these scammers. That is the purpose of this book, so the public is aware of this happening now. What have I learned is this is not going away anytime soon. They are hard to penetrate because they are a major, organized crime group. They work together to scam you by any means necessary to drain you of every last penny you own. They do not care if you are destitute or have any food to eat after they perform their scam, then move to the next victim. Most work on several victims at the same time, and sometimes you are dealing with multiple scammers at once. They stick to a storyline that they set up to scam you. There are multiple Yahoo Boy Facebook accounts that buy and sell storylines to use on unsuspecting victims. They also buy and sell their victims' personal information and continue to use them after they become useless to other scams. Some unsuspecting women become money mules and are used to perform scams on other victims or to launder money through their own personal bank accounts or to set up bank account for scammers to use for laundering money. Two hundred and one million dollars has been lost in romance scams here in the United States, and that is only 1 percent reporting their crimes. Can you imagine if all of us victims reported their crime? It is in the billions very easily, and that is one country. It means it is bigger than society knows. Why don't all report their crimes? They are devastated financially and emotionally; most are suicidal and want to keep it a secret from all their loved ones. I know I did! I was embarrassed and angered at what happened. You don't want to tell anyone! Most women will only discuss it with another victim, and most of us need some counseling but cannot afford it. Support groups are popping up, but some are not what they seem and badger women and are infiltrated by scammers too. I was in a support group at first like this. I ended it immediately and now joined a private group that works hard on filtering out people that have any connection still with scammers. It is where you can go to speak with another who suffered like you and hopefully have some peace of mind. Knowing you are not alone eases the suffering, and upholding one another strengthens us to move forward as human beings and pick up the pieces. I cannot stop a scammer, and I do not know the true identity of the man who scammed me either. I have no closure, only anger and regret. Had I known about Romance Scams and how they worked, I would not have been a victim. I am an intelligent woman, and so are most they choose to scam. Whatever the reason, I choose to fight, and advocacy is the key. Educating unsuspecting women and men on this subject can deter them from being a victim of this crime. The FBI will not investigate unless it is a large sum lost, and then they cannot locate the scammers, and there is no recovery of the money lost. FTC has a website, IC3.gov. It is an Internet Crime Complaint website. That is how you report your crime here in the United States. I urge every American victim to do so. Why? So they know the extent of these crimes and how bad it really is here. This is not going away and hopefully, through education and advocacy, can get under control. Typically, these scammers are from third-world countries. Nigeria is a mecca of romance scammers; they have cheap access to internet and can span the globe in using their resources to scam you. But they are not alone; Malaysia,

India, and other counties are where scammers reside. Even here in the United States they have contacts. They can find you and destroy your life from anywhere around the globe. Do not underestimate them. Do not try to scam them; they can devastate you. Playing with a scammer can cause you bodily harm to you or love ones. I have talked to women who tried, and some had their homes broken into along with death threats. Please heed these warnings as a precaution. I would have loved to take down my scammer and destroy him or them. But I am alone and will not risk my life to do so, and neither should any other victim. If you are a victim, please seek help in recovering from this crime. Scamhaters.com has a wealth of information, and you can message them for help or advice. I did, and these people are a nonprofit and work around the clock to help those of us who are victims. I talked with the administrator to this site, and she has given me permission to use them as a reference in this book. Google romance scams and see what information it provides. But, honestly, you do not realize the enormous number of victims this crime has taken until you become one yourself. I cannot tell you how many of us there are, but there are hundreds of thousands to date and growing. Imagine only 1 percent report their crimes. That means there are 99 percent of the victims that have suffered and do not speak openly; some never speak at all, and some have taken their lives. This is a heartbreaking crime unknown to the public, and most respond, "Well, she gave all her money willingly. She is stupid and gullible for doing so." But what if it happened to one of you or a loved one. Mother, sister, aunt, or grandmother, and she suffered alone because of the humiliation and judgement? How would you feel if she took her life because of this crime? These are questions to ask yourself before you pass judgement on me or other victims of this crime. I would want any victim of this crime to speak loud and proud about their story. This book has been gut wrenching and therapeutic for me because it showed me the red flags I missed and will allow me to put this in the past and emotionally and spiritually move forward. But I will carry the scars for life, because I will always be looking over my shoulder wondering when Erick Andersen will surface again. I will carry the antitrust scar that plagues so many of us victims. Why me? will always be an unanswered question, and that has left unresolved questions with no answers. I have had no contact with the other victim. I was said not to contact him because he is innocent, but maybe one day we will speak. I am not ready for that now but maybe in the future. When you work hard at putting a devastating crime behind you, reopening those wounds can be harmful. So, for now, I will not address that issue. I choose to move forward and find happiness in my lifetime. I am still an optimist but an educated one. I have so many people to thank for inspiration for this book. Those other victims are my heroes, and my heart bleeds for them to find a reason to move forward in their live. I hope this book has a positive impact on someone else's life. That they heed the warnings and are prevented from being another victim of these scammers and that maybe some legislation can be invoked into law to get social media to filter out these scammers, because that is where they thrive. They steal pictures from unsuspecting people and use them to scam and steal from victims. And to educate women on what to look out for when on social media pages. There are similarities in most all romance scams. For all of those women, and men too, who have fallen victim to this scam, please seek help, whether it is through a professional or a support group, and self-love is the key to regaining some stability in your life. My heart breaks for each and every victim these scammers have taken and continue to take. I hope that bringing awareness to this awful crime will shed light on the issue and will educate society as a whole that we are not stupid and gullible women who freely gave all we had. I want to thank every one of those who have advocated against romance scams. They continue to work relentlessly to educate and help victims who are desperately in need of help. What I want to see is legislation for all social media platforms to put restrictions in place from allowing your photos from being stolen from there page. I want them to take responsibility for allowing Yahoo Boys from setting up Facebook and Instagram pages recruiting others and sharing illegal information. I want all dating websites to screen all dating profiles and to educate all those seeking a profile how to detect scammers. Fake profiles and stolen information along with computer generated phone numbers non-VOIP (Voice Over Internet Protocol). These numbers need to be regulated or be limited in use.